TURKISH PHRASE BOOK

(Book & MP3-CD)

Necla Bal

Edited By Ceren Özler

ISBN 975-00271-0-8

www.onlineturkish.com
info@onlineturkish.com

çatıgrafik

Sinanpaşa Mah. Akmazçeşme Sk.
No: 19 K:3/4 Beşiktaş - İstanbul
tel: 0 212 260 92 32 (pbx)
fax: 0 212 260 92 33
e-mail: info@catigrafik.com
web: www.catigrafik.com

First Edition: August 2005

TURKISH PHRASE BOOK

The main goal of OnlineTurkish.com self study products is to help people who need to learn practical Turkish. Encouraging appropriate usage of words and phrases you already know, this phrase book is a helpful tool for learners like you to improve your speaking skills.

OnlineTurkish.com Turkish Phrase Book is not designed for teaching complete Turkish; however, it is designed for practicing commonly used words and phrases in daily life. OnlineTurkish.com Turkish Phrase Book contains more than two thousand and five hundred basic phrases and expressions used in daily life, such as in shopping, travel, banking etc. Also, with our Endearment & Love, Tender Words and Marriage Proposal sections you can now express your emotions or propose in Turkish. The accompanying MP3-CD includes all words and phrases in the book and it is recorded by a native actor to make sure that the pronunciation is perfect. Turkish Phrase Book encourages you to learn the correct pronunciations by first listening and then repeating each phrase.

MP3 files are recorded slightly slowly by our native actor if compared to normal speaking speeds of Turkish people. However, a special effort is shown not to alter the characteristics of the Turkish language. At first times, you may still find it difficult to understand what you hear. I recommend you to be patient, because to understand what is being said is as important as speaking fluently.

You can also find a Glossary section for E-Mail, Trade, Computer & Internet Terms etc. on the next pages.

Please have a look at the Suggestions & Warnings section if you are planning to travel to Turkey and to get more information about the lifestyle of Turkish People.

I hope this book will help everyone who is interested in improving their speaking skills.

Necla Bal

TURKISH PHRASE BOOK INDEX

Subjects	Page	Subjects	Page
• Accommodation	9	• Internal Body Parts	81
• Airport - Arriving	11	• Languages	82
• Airport - Departing	13	• Laundry	83
• Bank	15	• Luggage	86
• Basic Phrases, Requests & Thanks	18	• Marriage Proposal	89
• At the Beach	21	• Measures & Quantities	90
• Body Parts	23	• Medicine	91
• Booking - Room	24	• Money	93
• Breakdowns	26	• Numbers	96
• Bus	29	• Occupations & Jobs	97
• Camping	31	• Office	101
• Car Parts	35	• Payment	104
• Celebrations	36	• Petrol Station	107
• Clothes	38	• Pharmacy	109
• Colors	40	• Post Office	111
• Complaints	41	• Problems	115
• Country Names	44	• Reception	119
• Customs Control	45	• Rent a Car	122
• Days, Months & Seasons	47	• Restaurant	124
• Dental Problems	49	• Room Service	127
• Directions	51	• Shopping	129
• Diseases	54	• Shops A-Z	132
• Drinks	56	• Sightseeing in Istanbul	133
• Driving	58	• Signs & Notices	137
• Emergencies	61	• Stationery A-Z	139
• Endearment & Love	65	• Taxi	140
• Fax	67	• Telephone Call	142
• Food	69	• Television	145
• Fruits	71	• Tender Words	147
• Greetings	72	• Time Expressions	150
• Health Problems	74	• Train	151
• Hobbies & Interests	76	• Vegetables	154
• In a Hotel	79	• What Time Is It?	158

Suggestions and Warnings

Öneriler ve Uyarılar

INDEX

In this section you will find a short information about Turkey. Warnings and suggestions may help you if you intend to visit my country.

Subjects	Page
• Communication	160
• Cigarette Smoking	160
• Driving	161
• Electricity	161
• Food & Water	161
• Health	162
• Money & Valuables	162
• Photograph Taking	164
• Theft & Robbery	164
• Time Zone	164
• Tipping	165
• Toilets	165
• Transportation	165
• Visa	167
• What to Bring	167
• What to Buy	168
• Where to Go	169
• Weights & Measure	170

GLOSSARY

Terimler Sözlüğü

INDEX

Subjects	Page
• Glossary of Business & Economics Terms	171
• Glossary of Computer & Internet	194
• Glossary of E-Mail Terms	218
• Glossary of Nationalities	220
• Glossary of Trade & Import-Export Terms	223

Accommodation

Kalacak Yer

If you haven't booked accommodation in advance, local tourist offices have room-booking services or may help you to find a place.

a single room with bath	**banyolu tek kişilik oda**
a twin-bedded room	**çift kişilik yataklı oda**
accommodation	**kalacak yer**
breakfast	**kahvaltı**
book (v.)	**yer ayırtmak**
cheap	**ucuz**
cheaper	**daha ucuz**
confirm (v.)	**1. doğrulamak** **2. onaylamak**
full board	**tam pansiyon**
half board	**yarım pansiyon**
hotel	**otel**
How much?	**Ne kadar?**
next to each other	**yan yana**
no vacancy	**dolu**
opposite to each other	**karşılıklı**
sign (v.)	**imzalamak**
stay (v.)	**kalmak**
vacancy	**boş**

Q: Hello! Do you have a list of accommodations including prices?
Merhaba! Kalınabilecek yerler ve fiyatlarını içeren bir listeniz var mı?

A: Yes, here you are.
Evet, işte buyrun.

A: Sorry, we haven't.
Özür dilerim kalmamış.

Q: Excuse me! Do you know any hotel around here?
Özür dilerim! Buralarda bildiğiniz bir otel var mı?

A: Yes. You can find a good one at the right corner of the road.
Evet. Sokağın sağ köşesinde bir tane bulabilirsiniz.

Q: Can you suggest a good place for tonight?
Bu gece için kalacak iyi bir yer önerebilir misiniz?

A: Yes. I know a pretty hotel very close to here.
Evet. Buraya yakın sevimli bir otel biliyorum.

Q: Any vacancies for tonight?
Bu gece için boş yeriniz var mı?

A: Sorry, we're full up.
Özür dilerim, tamamıyla doluyuz.

Q: Do you have a room for tonight?
Bu gece için boş odanız var mı?

A: You are lucky, only one room is left.
Şanslısınız, sadece bir tane kaldı.

A: I wish a room having a sea view.
Denize bakan bir oda olsun isterdim.

* * * * * *

Q: I will send a fax. Do you have a fax machine?
Bir faks göndereceğim. Faks makineniz var mı?

A: Yes we have. Please ask for help from that young lady.
Evet var. Lütfen şu genç bayandan yardım isteyin.

A: Ok, thanks.
Peki, teşekkürler.

Airport Arriving

Hava Limanına Geliş

Turkish Airlines (THY) provide a vital network of domestic flights from the international airports.

Most signs at the airports of Turkey are in English and you may go through the airport without having to speak any Turkish. You can also use the ground handling service buses from airports to the centre of the cities. Here are some expressions you will find useful to know.

airport	**1. havaalanı** **2. havalimanı**
arrivals	**geliş**
baggage claim	**bagaj isteme**
boarding card	**biniş kartı**
boarding gate	**biniş kapısı**
car park	**araba parkı**
customs control	**gümrük kontrol**
departing	**1. hareket** **2. gidiş**
departures	**gidiş**
entrance	**giriş**
exit	**çıkış**
land (v.) (plane / aircraft)	**inmek** (uçak)
passport control	**pasaport kontrol**
plane	**uçak**
shuttle bus	**dahili servis**
take off (v.) (plane / aircraft)	**1. havalanmak** (uçak) **2. kalkmak** (uçak)

Q: Where is the luggage for the flight from Paris?
Paris uçağının bagajları nerede?

Q: Where can I get my luggage?
Bagajlarımı nereden alabilirim?

A: Go straight ahead and turn right please.
Doğru gidin ve sağa dönün lütfen.

Q: Is there an airport bus to the city centre?
Şehir merkezine otobüs var mı?

A: Yes. There are airport buses departing hourly.
Evet. Saat başı kalkan havaalanı otobüsleri var.

Q: Can we get into the bus now?
Otobüse şimdiden binebilir miyiz?

A: Sure. Please go to the exit.
Elbette. Lütfen çıkışa gidin.

Q: How much does it cost to take a taxi to downtown The Marmara hotel?
Şehir merkezindeki Marmara Otele taksi ne kadar tutar?

A: There are taximeters in front of taxi drivers. You can check the price.
Taksi şoförlerinin önünde taksimetreler vardır. Fiyatı kontrol edebilirsiniz.

Q: Is the town very far from the airport?
Şehir havaalanından çok uzakta mı?

A: Not really. It takes half an hour by taxi.
Pek değil. Taksi ile yarım saat sürer.

Q: How do I go to Izmir by bus?
İzmir'e otobüsle nasıl gidebilirim?

A: You have to go central garage.
Otobüs garajına gitmek zorundasınız.

Q: Where can I change some money?
Nerede döviz bozdurabilirim?

A: There are two banks near the exit for change.
Çıkışın yanında döviz bozdurabileceğiniz iki banka var.

A: Driver, please take me to The Marmara Hotel.
Şoför bey lütfen beni Marmara Oteli'ne götür.

Airport Departing

Havalimanından Hareket

Most signs at the airports of Turkey are in English and you may go through the airport without having to speak any Turkish. You can also use the ground handling service buses from airports to the centre of the cities. Here are some expressions you will find useful to know.

airport	**1. havaalanı** **2. havalimanı**
arrivals	**geliş**
baggage claim	**bagaj isteme**
boarding card	**biniş kartı**
boarding gate	**biniş kapısı**
car park	**araba parkı**
customs control	**gümrük kontrol**
departing	**1. hareket** **2. gidiş**
departures	**gidiş**
entrance	**giriş**
exit	**çıkış**
land (v.) (plane / aircraft)	**inmek** (uçak)
passport control	**pasaport kontrol**
plane	**uçak**
shuttle bus	**dahili servis**
take off (v.) (plane / aircraft)	**1. havalanmak** (uçak) **2. kalkmak** (uçak)

Q: What is the latest time I can check in?
En geç ne zaman "check in" yaptırabilirim?

A: Oh you are late! Go immediately to the counter A.
Oh geç kaldınız! Hemen A kontuarına gidin.

Q: Where do I check in for the flight to Antalya?
Antalya uçağı için nerede "check in" yaptıracağım?

Q: Which is the departure gate for the flight to Izmir?
İzmir uçağının bekleme salonu hangisi?

A: Boarding will take place at gate number 240.

Uçağa biniş 240 (iki yüz kırk) numaralı bekleme salonunda olacak.

A: It is up there.

O şurada.

A: Your flight is delayed.

Sizin uçağınız ertelendi.

A: Oh no! I am going to be late again for my meeting.

Ah hayır! Yine toplantıma geç kalacağım.

* * * * * *

Q: Can I help you?

Yardım edebilir miyim?

A: I'd like to reconfirm my flight to Ankara.

Ankara uçağına ayırttığım yeri yeniden onaylamak istiyorum.

Q: What is the matter?

Sorun nedir?

A: I want to change my booking.

Ben ayırttığım bileti değiştirmek istiyorum.

A: I want to cancel my booking.

Ayırttığım bileti iptal etmek istiyorum.

Bank

Banka

It is generally recommended not to change your money at the Airport (change only $20-30). You will get a better price at the exchange offices called "**Döviz Bürosu**". Check rates and compare. Do not try to change your money at local banks, they charge a commission. It is also recommended not to bring traveler's checks. You can have difficulties to cash them.

It's better to use cash; USD or EURO currencies. Turkish banks have the following working hours:

08:30 to 12:30

13:30 to 17:00

Banks are closed on Saturdays, Sundays and on official holidays.

ATMs of banks accept cards. All major credit cards are accepted. ATMs are widely available in large cities and tourist areas (including small towns). They usually do not let you to choose language to carry out the transaction. Furthermore, in smaller places, you might have trouble finding one that takes your card. Machines are not always reliable, so it is advisable to carry an extra day's cash. If one bank's ATM is not working, other banks nearby may well remain operational.

account	**1. hesap** **2. banka hesabı**
ATM	**ATM**
bank	**banka**
bank notes	**kağıt para**
cash	**nakit para**
cash dispenser	**ATM**
cashier	**kasiyer**
credit card	**kredi kartı**
checking account	**cari hesap**
deposit (v.)	**yatırmak** (bankaya)
identity card	**kimlik kartı**
payment	**ödeme**
savings account	**tasarruf hesabı**
small change	**bozuk para**

cash (v.)	**1. paraya çevirmek** **2. bozdurmak**
pay (v.)	**ödemek**
settle (pay) (v.)	**ödemek**
swallow (v.)	**yutmak**
tourist check	**turist çeki**
traveler's checks (US) traveller's cheques (UK)	**seyahat çeki**
windows	**1. gişe** **2. pencere**

Q: Hello. Will you please change this traveler's check?
Merhaba. Şu seyahat çeklerini bozar mısınız lütfen?

A: Ok. Be quick please. We are going to be closed soon.
Peki. Biraz hızlı olun lütfen. Kapanmak üzereyiz.

Q: What rate have you given me?
Bana hangi kurdan veriyorsunuz?

A: We use the Central Bank rates.
Biz Merkez Bankası kurunu uygularız.

A: You have given me a very low rate.
Siz çok düşük bir kur uyguladınız.

Q: Sorry, I have nothing to do.
Özür dilerim, yapabileceğim başka bir şey yok.

A: Please give me large notes.
Lütfen bana bütün para verin.

A: OK. Here you are.
Peki. İşte paranız.

Q: Furthermore, can you change these notes into local currency?
Ayrıca şu parayı yerel paraya çevirir misiniz?

A: Please go to the exchange window.
Lütfen döviz bozdurma gişesine gidin.

Q: Where's the exchange window?
Döviz gişesi nerede?

A: It is up there. Please be quick.
İşte şurada. Lütfen çabuk olun.

Q: Shall I have to wait long?
Çok bekleyecek miyim?

A: Sorry, madam. We are closed.
Özür dilerim hanımefendi. Biz kapandık.

* * * * * *

A: Excuse me! The cash dispenser has swallowed my credit card.
Özür dilerim. ATM makinesi kredi kartımı yuttu.

Q: Would you please go to the complaints department?
Lütfen şikayet departmanına gider misiniz?

A: Here you are. Your credit card Sir.
İşte kredi kartınız beyefendi.

Q: Can I use my card with this cash dispenser again?
Kartımı aynı makinede yeniden deneyebilir miyim?

A: Sure. Try it one more time.
Elbette. Bir kere daha deneyin.

Q: Can I use my credit card to get Swiss Franks?
Kartımla İsviçre Frangı çekebilir miyim?

A: Yes you can.
Evet çekebilirsiniz.

* * * * * *

Q: Hello, could you tell me whether you have received a transfer from Switzerland for Danny White?
Merhaba, İsviçre'den Danny White için bir havale geldi mi?

Q: How much it was?
Ne kadardı?

A: Thirty thousand Swiss Franks from the National Bank.
National Bank'tan otuz bin İsviçre Frangı.

Q: Yes we have. May I have your identity card?
Evet geldi. Kimliğinizi verir misiniz?

A: Here you are my passport.
İşte pasaportum.

Q: Can I pay with US Dollars?
Dolar olarak ödeyebilir miyim?

A: Yes you can.
Evet, ödeyebilirsiniz.

Q: Do you have any change?
Bozuk paranız var mı?

A: Thank you.
Teşekkür ederim.

Basic Phrases, Requests & Thanks

Basit İfadeler, Rica ve Teşekkür

Excuse me! (to catch attention)	**Afedersiniz!**
Excuse me. (sorry)	**Afedersiniz.**
Madam / Mrs. / Ms.	**Bayan**
Many thanks!	**Çok teşekkürler!**
No.	**Hayır.**
Okay.	**1. Peki.** **2. Tamam.**
Pardon?	**1. Efendim?** **2. Pardon?**
Please.	**Lütfen.**
Sir / Mr.	**Bay**
Sorry!	**1. Özür dilerim!** **2. Pardon!**
Thank you.	**Teşekkür ederim.**
Thanks a lot!	**Çok teşekkürler!**
Thank you very much.	**Çok teşekkürler.**
Thanks!	**Teşekkürler!**
No thanks!	**Hayır, teşekkür ederim!**

Note: "Teşekkürler!" in response to an offer usually means "No thanks!" If you want to indicate a positive response to an offer, say "Evet, lütfen!" or "Evet, teşekkür ederim."

Yes.	**Evet.**
Yes, please!	**Evet, lütfen!**

Q: Do you speak Turkish?
Türkçe konuşur musunuz?
Türkçe biliyor musunuz?

A: No, I don't.
Hayır.

Q: Do you speak English?
İngilizce konuşur musunuz?

A: Yes I do.
Evet.

Q: Do you speak German?
Almanca biliyor musunuz?

A: I speak very little German.
Çok az Almanca biliyorum.

Q: What is "apple" called in German?
Almanca "elma" nasıl denir?

A: I don't know.
Bilmiyorum.

Q: Do you understand my words?
Sözlerimi anlıyor musunuz?

A: I don't understand you.
Sizi anlamıyorum.

Q: Could you repeat that please? Ok, thank you.
Şunu tekrar edebilir misiniz? Peki, teşekkürler.

A: You're welcome!
Bir şey değil. (In response to "Thank you!)

Q: Can I help you?
Yardım edebilir miyim?

A: No, thanks!
Hayır, teşekkürler!

Q: Can you help me?
Yardım edebilir misiniz?

A: Sure.
Elbette.

Q: May I have the salt please?
Tuzu alabilir miyim lütfen?

Q: Here you are.
Buyrun.
Alın.

Q: Would you please give me that book?
Lütfen, şu kitabı bana verir misiniz?

Q: Pardon? What would you like?
Pardon! Ne istemiştiniz?

Q: Excuse me, where is the toilet?
Afederiniz, tuvalet nerede?

A: It is at the end of the corridor.
Koridorun sonunda.

Q: Ok, thank you.
Peki, teşekkür ederim.

At the Beach

Sahilde

There are thousands of natural beaches along Black Sea, Marmara Sea, Aegean Sea and Mediterranean Sea. I also suggest visitors to attend a Blue Voyage to discover the islands and coasts embraced with history and nature by this fantastic boat cruise.

bathing suite / swimsuit	**mayo**
bikini	**bikini**
boat	**1. sandal** **2. kayık** **3. tekne**
deck chair	**şezlong**
fishing (n.)	**balık avlama**
sand	**kum**
sea	**deniz**
springboard	**sıçrama tahtası**
sunburn	**güneş yanığı**
sunglasses	**güneş gözlüğü**
sunshade	**1. güneş şemsiyesi** **2. güneşlik**
swim (v.)	**yüzmek**
swimming pool	**yüzme havuzu**
tent	**1. çadır** **2. tente**
wave	**dalga**
wave (v.)	**el sallamak**

Q: Are there any good beaches near here?
Buralarda güzel bir plaj var mı?

A: Yes. There is one opposite of the Blue Hotel.
Evet. Blue Hotel'in karşısında bir tane var.

Q: Is there a swimming pool for children?
Çocuklar için bir yüzme havuzu var mı?

A: Yes. There is a small one near the beach.
Evet. Plajın yanında küçük bir tane var.

Q: Where can I hire a boat?
Nereden sandal kiralayabilirim?

A: Please ask for the pay-desk at the entrance of the beach.
Lütfen plaj girişindeki ödeme gişesine sorun.

Q: How much is these sunglasses?
Bu güneş gözlükleri kaç lira?

A: A hundred and fifty Liras each.
Tanesi yüz elli Lira.

Q: Would you please bring us one more deck chair?
Lütfen bir tane daha şezlong getirir misiniz?

A: Sorry all are occupied now. I will bring if one becomes free.
Özür dilerim, şu anda hepsi dolu. Biri boşalırsa getiririm.

Q: Where can we have a shower?
Nerede duş alabiliriz?

A: The showers are at the exit of the beach.
Duşlar plajın çıkışında.

Q: The water is polluted isn't it?
Deniz kirli değil mi?

A: Yes, it is also choppy today.
Evet, aynı zamanda çırpıntılı.

A: It's dangerous to swim today.
Bugün yüzmek tehlikeli.

A: Let's lay down on the sand and have a sunbath.
En iyisi kumlara uzanıp, güneş banyosu yapalım.

Body Parts

Vücut Bölümleri

abdomen	**karın**
ankle	**ayak bileği**
arm	**kol**
back	**sırt**
bone	**kemik**
calf	**baldır**
cheek	**yanak**
chest	**göğüs**
chin	**çene**
ear	**kulak**
elbow	**dirsek**
eye	**göz**
eyebrow	**kaş**
finger	**el parmağı**
foot	**ayak**
hair	**saç**
hand	**el**
head	**1. baş** **2. kafa**
hip	**kalça**
joint	**eklem**
knee	**1. diz** **2. diz kapağı**
leg	**bacak**
lip	**dudak**
mouth	**ağız**
nail	**tırnak**
neck	**boyun**
nose	**burun**
throat	**boğaz**
thumb	**başparmak**
toe	**ayak parmağı**
tooth	**diş**
waist	**bel**

Booking a Room in a Hotel

Otelde Yer Ayırtmak

A room at the backside.	**Arkaya bakan bir oda.**
A single room with shower.	**Duşlu tek kişilik oda.**
A twin-bedded quiet room.	**Çift kişilik sakin bir oda.**
We'd like rooms next to each other.	**Yan yana iki oda istiyoruz.**
With an extra bed for a child.	**Ekstra çocuk yataklı oda.**

Q: Hello! This is Robert Black. Do you have any vacancies?
Alo! Benim adım Robert Black. Boş odanız var mı?

A: Hello Mr. Black. Unfortunately, we're full up.
Merhaba Mr. Black. Neyazık ki tamamıyla doluyuz.

Q: Ok. Can you give me the phone number of another hotel?
Peki. Başka bir otelin telefonunu verebilir misiniz?

A: Please try +90 212 594 00 00.
Lütfen +90 212 594 00 00 'ı deneyin.

Q: Hello! +90 212 594 00 00?
Alo! Doksan-iki yüz on iki-beş yüz doksandört-çift sıfır-çift sıfır mı? (+90 212 594 00 00)

Q: Yes sir. Who is speaking?
Evet bayım. Kimsiniz?

A: This is Robert Black. I'd like to book a room.
Ben Robert Black. Bir oda ayırtmak istiyorum.

Q: For how many nights?
Kaç gecelik?

A: We'd like to stay four nights from ... till/to ...
Biz ... tarihinden ... tarihine kadar dört gece kalmak istiyoruz.

Q: How much is it, per night I mean?
Fiyatı ne kadar, yani geceliği?

A: Fifty USD per night.
Geceliği elli Dolar.

Q: Is breakfast included?
Kahvaltı dahil mi?

Q: How much is it for half board and full board?
Tam ve yarım pansiyon fiyatları ne kadar?

A: 65 USD for half board and 105 USD for full board.
Yarım pansiyon (65) altmış beş, tam pansiyon (105) yüz beş Dolar.

A: Ok. I prefer half board.
Peki. Ben yarım pansiyon tercih ederim.

A: Yes sir. I've booked a room for that name Robert Black.
Peki efendim. Robert Black adına bir oda ayırdım.

A: Please confirm your reservation via e-mail or fax.
Lütfen e- mail veya faksla rezervasyonunuzu onaylayın.

Breakdowns

Aksilikler

battery	**pil**
break down (v.)	**1. bozulmak** **2. arıza yapmak**
engine	**1. motor** **2. makina**
flat tire	**patlak lastik**
garage	**garaj**
get off (v.)	**çıkarmak**
leak (v.)	**sızdırmak**
overheating	**hararet yapmak**
part	**parça**
petrol station	**1. benzin istasyonu** **2. benzinci**
pull (v.)	**çekmek**
push (v.)	**itmek**
run out (v.) (of petrol etc.)	**bitmek (benzin vs.)**
start (v.)	**çalıştırmak**
the nearest	**en yakın**
water	**su**
wheel	**tekerlek**
windscreen	**ön cam**

Q: Excuse me! Can you help me?
Afedersiniz! Yardım eder misiniz?

A: Sorry, I can't understand your language.
Özür dilerim, dilinizi anlamıyorum.

A: My car has broken down.
Arabam arızalandı.

A: As I understand your car has a problem.
Anladığım kadarıyla arabanızda bir problem var.

Q: Can you give me a push?
Arkadan itebilir misiniz?

A: Just a moment. I'll try to start it.
Bir dakika. Çalıştırmayı deneyeceğim.

A: The car doesn't start.
Araba çalışmıyor.

Q: Is there a mechanic near here?
Yakında bir tamirci var mı?

A: There is no problem with your car. You have run out of petrol.
Arabanızda problem yok. Benzininiz bitmiş.

Q: Petrol? Oh my God! What shall I do now?
Benzin? Aman Allahım! Ben şimdi ne yapacağım?

A: Do not panic please.
Panik yapmayın lütfen.

Q: Is there a gas station near here?
Yakında bir benzinci var mı?

A: Please walk about one kilometer. Buy a can of petrol.
Buradan bir kilometre kadar yürüyün. Bir bidon benzin alın.

A: OK. Thanks. You are so kind.
Peki. Teşekkürler. Çok naziksiniz.

Q: What is going on there? Can I help you?
Orada neler oluyor? Yardım edebilir miyim?

A: I have a flat tire. I can't get the tire off.
Lastiğim patladı. Tekerleği sökemiyorum.

Q: Would you please let me try?
Denememe izin verir misiniz?

A: Ok. Thanks.
Peki. Teşekkür ederim.

Q: Are you sure that the only problem is the flat tire?
Tek problemin lastikte olduğundan emin misiniz?

Q: What do you mean?
Ne demek istediniz?

A: I suppose your petrol tank is leaking.
Sanırım benzin deponuzda sızıntı var.

Q: Really! Where is the nearest petrol station?
Gerçekten mi! En yakın petrol istasyonu nerede?

A: It is quite far.
Epey uzak.

Q: Can you help me?
Yardım eder misiniz?

A: I am in a hurry now.
Benim şu anda acelem var.

A: I can send you a taxi. OK?
Size bir taksi gönderirim. Tamam mı?

Q: Many thanks. Please send me a taxi as soon as possible.
Çok teşekkürler. Lütfen en kısa zamanda bir taksi gönderin.

A: Taxi! Please take me to the nearest petrol station.
Taksi! Lütfen beni en yakın benzinciye götürün.

* * * * * *

A: My car has broken down.
Benim arabam bozuldu.

Q: What is the problem?
Problem nedir?

A: My tank is leaking.
Depom benzin sızdırıyor.

Q: Where is your car?
Arabanız nerede?

A: It is on the highway.
Anayolda.

A: Ok. Get on my car. I'll have a look at it.
Peki. Benim arabama binin. Ben ona bir bakayım.

A: No problem with your petrol tank. Your engine is overheating.
Benzin deponuzda problem yok. Motor hararet yapmış.

Q: Really?
Gerçekten mi?

A: It just needs water. I'll add some water to your radiator.
Sadece suya ihtiyacı var. Radyatörünüze su ekleyeceğim.

A: Sorry. I have caused a lot of trouble to you. Many thanks.
Özür dilerim. Size çok zahmet verdim. Çok teşekkürler.

Bus

Otobüs

If you are planning to use public transport, it's more practical to buy a smart ticket, **Ak-bil**. You can use it either at the bus stops or at the metro stations. There are no discount options for tourists or families.

art gallery	**sanat galerisi**
bus	**otobüs**
bus stop	**otobüs durağı**
get off (v.) (bus /car / bicycle / train / plane / horse etc.)	**inmek** (otobüs / araba / bisiklet / tren / uçak / at vs.)
get on (v.) (bus / car / bicycle / train / plane / horse etc.)	**binmek** (otobüs / araba / bisiklet / tren / uçak / at vs.)
museum	**müze**
out of the bus	**otobüsün dışında**
station	**istasyon**
take a taxi (v.)	**taksi tutmak**

Q: Is there a bus to...?
...'e /'a otobüs bulunur mu?

To show directions **-e** or **-a** are added to the end of names of places according to the Vowel Harmony Rule. These suffixes are used instead of **to** in English. They are separated by an apostrophe when added to the end of private names. The suffixes **-den** and **-dan** are used instead of **from** according to Vowel Harmony Rule.

Examples:

Q: Is there a bus **to** Sultanahmet?
Sultanahmet'**e** otobüs bulunur mu?

Q: Is there a bus **to** Boshporus?
İstanbul Boğazın'**a** otobüs bulunur mu?

A: Where does the bus **to** Yesilkoy take off?
Yeşilköy'**e** otobüs nereden kalkar?

Q: Where can I buy tickets? **On** the bus?
Biletleri nereden alabilirim? Otobüs**te** mi?

A: You can buy them **from** the ticket offices at the main bus stops.
Biletleri ana duraklardaki gişeler**den** alabilirsiniz.

Q: How much does it cost **to** Taksim?
Taksim'e ne kadar tutar?

A: It is seventy five Kuruş.
Yetmişbeş Kuruş.

Q: How often are the buses **to** Hisar?
Hisar'**a** hangi sıklıkta otobüs kalkar?

A: Every half an hour.
Her yarım saate bir.

Q: How many hours does it take from Taksim to Yesilkoy?
Taksim'**den** Yeşilköy'**e** ne kadar zamanda gidilir?

A: Please tell me when to get off.
Lütfen ne zaman ineceğimi bana söyleyin.

Q: When is the first bus to Ortakoy?
Ortaköy'**e** ilk otobüs ne zaman?

Q: When is the last bus to Kadikoy?
Kadıköy'**e** son otobüs ne zaman?

A: The first bus is at 06.00 o'clock to Ortakoy.
Ortaköy'**e** ilk otobüs 06.00'dadır.

A: Please! I want to get off.
Lütfen! İnmek istiyorum.

Q: What is the matter?
Sorun nedir?

A: I suppose I missed my stop.
Sanırım ineceğim durağı kaçırdım.

A: This is my stop.
Bu benim durağım.

Q: Can I help you?
Yardım edebilir miyim?

A: How can I get to the nearest bus stop?
En yakın otobüs durağına nasıl giderim?

Camping

Kamp Yapmak

Many tour agencies organize trekking expeditions, river rafting and horseback trips for the adventurous travelers. Fully equipped campers (caravans) can be rented in the major cities for excursions to the countryside. There are also forest camps of The Ministry of Forestry. You can have details of the campsites and prices from local Turkish Tourism Offices.

air-bed	**havalı yatak**	lantern	**fener**
barbecue	**barbekü**	lend (v.)	**ödünç vermek**
blanket	**battaniye**	mat	**1. mat 2. altlık**
boot	**1. çizme 2. bot**	no camping area	**kamp yapılmaz**
camp (v.)	**kamp yapmak**	overnight	**gecelik**
camp fire	**kamp ateşi**	per night	**1. gecelik 2. gece başına**
camper	**kampçı**	raincoat	**yağmurluk**
campsite	**1. kamp 2. kamp yeri**	rope	**1. ip 2. halat**
caravan	**karavan**	rucksack / bacpack	**sırt çantası**
close	**yakın**	shelter	**korunak**
compass	**pusula**	shower	**duş**
electricity	**elektrik**	sleeping bag	**uyku tulumu**
far	**uzak**	stay (v.)	**kalmak**
flashlight	**el feneri**	tent	**çadır**
hammer	**çekiç**	thermos	**termos**
hot water	**sıcak su**	toilet	**tuvalet**
include	**dahil**	vacancy	**1. boş yer 2. yer**
lamp	**lamba**	wood	**odun**

Q: Do you have a list of campsites with prices?
Kamp yerlerinin fiyatlarını gösteren bir listeniz var mı?

A: Yes we have. Here you are.
Evet var. İşte buyrun.

Q: Is this campsite sheltered?
Bu kamp yeri korunaklı mı?

A: Yes it is.
Evet.

Q: Which one is close to sea?
Hangisi denize daha yakın?

A: This is really a good campsite near the sea.
Bu denize yakın iyi bir kamptır.

Q: How far is the sea?
Deniz ne kadar uzakta?

A: Very close.
Hemen bitişiğinde.

Q: Does it have a restaurant?
Lokantası var mı?

A: Sure.
Elbette.

Q: Is there a shop also?
Dükkan da var mı?

A: Yes, there is a small shop, too.
Evet, küçük bir dükkan da var.

* * * * *

Q: Do you have any vacancies?
Boş yeriniz var mı?

A: Yes we have.
Evet var.

Q: Can we hire a tent?
Bir çadır kiralayabilir miyiz?

A: Sure. Welcome to our camp.
Elbette. Kampımıza hoş geldiniz.

Q: How much is it per night for a tent?
Çadırların geceliği ne kadar?

Q: It is ten Liras. For how many nights?
On Lira. Kaç gece kalacaksınız?

Q: Can we camp here overnight?
Bir geceliğine kalabilir miyiz?

A: Why not! May I have your passports please?
Neden olmasın. Pasaportlarınızı alabilir miyim lütfen?

Q: Are there showers?
Duş var mı?

A: They are near the seaside.
Onlar deniz kıyısında.

Q: Is electricity included in the price?
Elektrik fiyatlara dahil mi?

A: Yes.
Evet.

Q: Can we pitch the tent here?
Çadırımızı şuraya kurabilir miyiz?

A: I suggest you to pitch it up under that olive tree.
Ben size şu zeytin ağacının altını öneririm.

Q: I am sorry! Where are the toilets?
Pardon! Tuvaletler nerede?

A: They are near the restaurant.
Onlar restoranın yanında.

Q: Is there a socket for the electric razor?
Orada tıraş makinesi için fiş var mı?

A: Yes, there are.
Evet, var.

Q: Is this water drinkable?
Bu su içilebilir mi?

A: Unfortunately not. You can buy the drinking water from the shop.
Ne yazık ki hayır. İçecek suyu bakkaldan satın alabilirsiniz.

Q: Could you lend me a hammer please?
Bana bir çekiç ödünç verebilir misiniz?

A: Here you are.
Buyrun.

Q: Where can we buy drinks?
İçecekleri nereden alabiliriz?

A: There is all kind of drinks at the bar.
Barda her türlü içki var.

Q: Can we make a fire?
Ateş yakabilir miyiz?

A: It is allowed only on the beach.
Sadece kumsalda yakılmasına izin veriliyor.

Car Parts

Araba Parçaları

accelerator	**gaz pedalı**
back seat	**arka koltuk**
battery	**akü**
bonnet	**kaput**
brake	**fren**
central locking	**merkezi kilit**
choke (v.)	**boğulmak**
clutch (n.)	**kavrama**
dashboard	**gösterge tablosu**
distributor	**distribütör**
engine	**motor**
exhaust pipe	**egzoz borusu**
fan belt	**pervane kayışı**
fog light	**sis lambası**
front seat	**ön koltuk**
fuse	**sigorta**
gear	**vites**
handbrake	**el freni**
headlights	**far**
ignition	**1. kontak** **2. ateşleme**
indicator	**sinyal**
points	**makas**
radiator	**radyatör**
rear lights	**arka lambalar**
rear view mirror	**dikiz aynası**
resistance	**rezistans**
reverse gear	**geri vitesi**
seat belt	**kemer**
spare wheel	**yedek lastik**
spark plug	**buji**
tire	**lastik**
wheel	**direksiyon**
windscreen	**ön cam**
wiper	**silecek**

Celebrations

Kutlamalar

Although, Gregorian calendar is used since 1 Jan 1927 the religious fests are celebrated according to Islam calendar in Turkey. As a consequence, the religious festivals are not celebrated on the same day every year because they are calculated according to the Islam calendar called "**Kameri Takvim**". Islam calendar is approximately 10 days shorter than the Christian year so the religious festival of Greater Bairam and the holy month of Ramadan circulate throughout the Christian year.

Ramadan and Greater Bairam (Sacrifice Fest) are the most important religious festivals in all Muslim countries. If you really wish to celebrate a religious fest of a friend, I suggest you to visit the following link:
http://www.earthcalendar.net/
You can also get more information about religious fests by visiting **http://www.kultur.gov.tr/portal/kultur_en.asp?belgeno=5656.**

All other fests and holidays are celebrated according to the Gregorian calendar. Here are a list of **Holidays and Fests for Turkey**:

New Year's Day	**December 31** / 31 Aralık	Yılbaşı
Children's Day / National Sovereignty	**April 23** / 23 Nisan	1. Çocuk Bayramı 2. Milli Egemenlik Bayramı
Hidirellez Festival *	**May 6** / 6 Mayıs	Hıdırellez*
Mother's Day*	**The 2nd Sunday of May** / Mayıs 2.Pazar	Anneler Günü*
Youth & Sports Day	**May 19** / 19 Mayıs	Gençlik ve Spor Bayramı
Victory Day	**August 30** / 30 Ağustos	Zafer Bayramı
Republic Day	**October 29** / 29 Ekim	Cumhuriyet Bayramı

***Note:**

Hidirellez Festival - not a holiday but celebrated by people as a Spring Fest. To get more info please visit:

http://www.kulturturizm.gov.tr/portal/kultur_tr.asp?belgeno=4530

May 11- **Mother's Day** is also not a holiday.

I'd like to wish you a merry Christmas.

Sana iyi Noel'ler dilerim.

Merry Christmas!

İyi Noeller!

Happy New Year!

Mutlu Yıllar!

I wish you a happy new year for you and your family.

Size ve ailenize mutlu yıllar dilerim.

I wish you the best of luck in the New Year!

Yeni yılın şans getirmesini dilerim!

All the best in the New Year!

En iyi dileklerimle yeni yılını kutlarım!

Happy Easter!

Mutlu Paskalyalar!

Happy birthday!

Doğum günün kutlu olsun!

Have a good trip!

İyi yolculuklar!

Best wishes!

En iyi dileklerimle!

Welcome!

Hoş geldiniz! [formal]
Hoş geldin! [informal]

Enjoy your meal!

Afiyet olsun!

Cheers!

Şerefe!

To your health!

Sağlığına!

Congratulations! (Passing an exam, getting married, etc.)
Tebrikler!

I wish a happy Ramadan to you.

Ramazan bayramınızı kutlar, nice mutlu bayramlar dilerim.

I wish you a happy Greater Bairam (Sacrifice Fest).

Kurban Bayramınızı kutlar, nice mutlu bayramlar dilerim.
İyi Bayramlar! (A term for general greeting of all fests.)

Clothes

Giyecekler

belt	**kemer**	shirt	**gömlek**
bikini	**bikini**	shoe	**ayakkabı**
blouse	**buluz**	shorts	**şort**
bra	**sütyen**	skirt	**etek**
coat	**ceket**	slippers	**terlik**
dress	**1. elbise** **2. giysi**	socks	**çorap**
gloves	**eldiven**	suit (for men)	**1. takım** **2. takım elbise**
hat	**şapka**	suit (for women)	**1. takım** **2. döpiyes**
jacket	**ceket**	swimsuit / bathing suit	**mayo**
knickers (women)	**1. külot** **2. kadın külodu**	tie	**kravat**
nightgown / nightdress	**gecelik**	tights	**külotlu çorap**
overcoat / coat	**palto**	tracksuit	**eşofman**
pullover	**kazak**	trousers / pants	**pantolon**
pajamas	**pijama**	t-shirt	**tişört**
raincoat	**yağmurluk**	underpants (for men)	**1. külot** **2. don**
sandals	**1. sandal** **2. sandalet**	waistcoat	**yelek**
scarf	**1. eşarp** **2. atkı** **3. kaşkol**		

Women's and Men's Suits

Women's Size	
UK & USA	EC & Turkey
10	36
12	38
14	40
16	42
18	44
20	46

Men's Size	
UK & USA	EC & Turkey
10	36
12	38
14	40
16	42
18	44
20	46

Shoes Size

Women's Size	
UK & USA	EC & Turkey
10	36
12	38
14	40
16	42
18	44
20	46

Men's Size	
UK & USA	EC & Turkey
10	36
12	38
14	40
16	42
18	44
20	46

Colors

Renklер

white	**beyaz**
black	**siyah**
red	**kırmızı**
yellow	**sarı**
blue	**mavi**
orange	**turuncu**
green	**yeşil**
purple	**mor**
brown	**kahverengi**
pink	**pembe**
grey	**gri**
dark blue	**lacivert**

Complaints

Şikayetler

complaint	**şikayet**
cold	**soğuk**
heating	**ısıtma**
hot	**sıcak**
large	**geniş**
light	**1. lamba** **2. ışık**
lock	**kilit**
noisy	**gürültülü**
small	**küçük**
tight	**dar**
work (v.)	**1. işlemek** **2. çalışmak**

Q: To whom can I complain? My goods were damaged in transit.
Eşyalarım taşınırken hasar görmüş. Kime şikayet edebilirim?

A: Please go to the complaints department.
Lütfen şikayet bürosuna başvurun.

Q: Can you help me? My goods were damaged in transit.
Yardım edebilir misiniz? Eşyalarım taşınırken hasar görmüş.

A: Ok. Fill the form for your complaints. Your loss will be paid off by our France company.
Tamam. Şu formu doldurun. Kaybınız sigorta şirketimiz tarafından ödenecektir.

* * * * * *

A: There's a problem with the room lights.
Odamdaki ışıklarda bir problem var.

Q: Really! What is the problem?
Gerçekten mi? Problem nedir?

A: The switches don't work.
Elektrik düğmeleri çalışmıyor.

Q: Did you try to plug it in. Ok. I am coming.
Fişi takmayı denediniz mi? Tamam. Ben geliyorum.

A: Thanks a lot.
Çok teşekkürler.

Q: Anything else?
Başka bir şey var mı?

A: It's too noisy. Why?
Çok gürültü var. Neden?

A: Oh, sorry. A new group has just came in. It will be over in minutes.
A, özür dilerim. Yeni bir grup geldi. Birkaç dakika içinde sona erer.

A: Ok. Thanks.
Peki. Teşekkürler.

* * * * * *

A: Waiter!
Garson!

Q: What is the matter Sir?
Sorun nedir efendim?

A: We have been waiting for a very long time.
Biz uzun zamandır bekliyoruz.

A: Your order will be ready soon. I am going to check.
Siparişiniz hazırlanmak üzeredir. Ben gidip siparişinize bir bakayım.

A: OK!
Peki.

Q: Sorry for the delay. Anything else?
Gecikme için özür dilerim. Başka bir arzunuz var mı?

A: Oh! This isn't what I ordered.
A! Ben bunları sipariş etmedim.

Q: I am terribly sorry. I am going to check your order again.
Çok çok özür dilerim. Şimdi gidip tekrar bakacağım.

A: OK! Thanks.
Peki. Teşekkürler.

Q: Anything else Sir?
Başka bir arzunuz var mı efendim?

A: The bill is not correct.
Faturada hata var.

A: Let me have a check. Oh yes, you are right. I am going to prepare a new bill for you.
Verin kontrol edeyim. Ah evet, haklısınız. Hemen yeni bir fatura düzenleyeyim.

A: Thanks a lot.
Çok teşekkürler.

* * * * * *

Q: Can you help me?
Yardım edebilir misiniz?

A: The zip doesn't work.
Fermuar çalışmıyor.

Q: Sorry. I am going to bring another skirt. Ok?
Özür dilerim. Size yeni bir etek getiriyorum. Olur mu?

A: But this is not the same color.
Fakat bu aynı renk değil.

Q: Pink fits you better than blue. Don't you think so?
Pembe renk size maviden daha çok yakıştı. Sizce de öyle değil mi?

A: Sorry. I do not want the pink one. I want my money back.
Özür dilerim. Ben pembe istemiyorum. Ben paramı geri istiyorum.

A: Ok. Follow me please. You have to go the returns department.
Peki. Lütfen beni takip edin. İade bölümüne gitmeniz gerekiyor.

Country Names

Ülke Adları

Afghanistan	**Afganistan**	Italy	**İtalya**
Albania	**Arnavutluk**	Japan	**Japonya**
Algeria	**Cezayir**	Jordan	**Ürdün**
Argentina	**Arjantin**	Kazakhstan	**Kazakistan**
Armenia	**Ermenistan**	Kyrgyzstan	**Kırgızistan**
Australia	**Avustralya**	Lebanon	**Lübnan**
Austria	**Avusturya**	Libya	**Libya**
Azerbaijan	**Azerbaycan**	Luxembourg	**Luksemburg**
Belgium	**Belçika**	Mexico	**Meksika**
Bolivia	**Bolivya**	Netherlands	**Hollanda**
Brazil	**Brezilya**	North Korea	**Kuzey Kore**
Bulgaria	**Bulgaristan**	Norway	**Norveç**
Canada	**Kanada**	Poland	**Polonya**
China	**Çin**	Portugal	**Portekiz**
Colombia	**Kolombiya**	Romania	**Romanya**
Cuba	**Küba**	Russia	**Rusya**
Cyprus	**Kıbrıs**	Saudi Arabia	**Suudi Arabistan**
Czech Republic	**Çek Cumhuriyeti**	South Africa	**Güney Afrika**
Denmark	**Danimarka**	South Korea	**Güney Kore**
Egypt	**Mısır**	Spain	**İspanya**
Finland	**Finlandiya**	Sweden	**İsveç**
France	**Fransa**	Switzerland	**İsviçre**
Germany	**Almanya**	Syria	**Suriye**
Greece	**Yunanistan**	Tajikistan	**Tacikistan**
Hong Kong	**Honkong**	Tunisia	**Tunus**
Hungary	**Macaristan**	Turkey	**Türkiye**
India	**Hindistan**	Turkmenistan	**Türkmenistan**
Indonesia	**Endonezya**	UK	**İngiltere**
Iran	**İran**	United States of America	**AmerikaBirleşik Devletleri**
Iraq	**Irak**	Uzbekistan	**Özbekistan**
Ireland	**İrlanda**	Venezuela	**Venezuella**
Israel	**İsrail**	Yugoslavia	**Yugoslavya**

Customs Control

Gümrük Kontrolü

If you are unsure of certain items in your luggage, check it at The Customs Office to see whether the tax payment is required.

bag	**çanta**
briefcase	**evrak çantası**
camera	**kamera**
customs	**gümrük vergisi**
customs officer	**gümrük memuru**
documents	**belgeler**
identity document	**kimlik kartı**
luggage	**bagaj**
papers	**evrak**
passport	**pasaport**
passport control	**pasaport kontrol**
policeman	**polis**
policewoman	**bayan polis**
porter	**hamal**
suitcase	**bavul**
traveler	**yolcu**
video camera	**video kamera**
visa	**vize**

A: Passports please.
Pasaport lütfen!

Q: Here you are. Do I have to pay tax for this?
Buyrun. Buna vergi ödemek zorunda mıyım?

A: Yes Sir.
Evet Bayım.

Q: It is for my own personal use. Do I need to pay the tax?
Fakat bu benim kişisel eşyam. Yine de vergi gerekli mi?

A: Unfortunately yes.
Ne yazık ki evet.

Q: How much tax must I pay?
Ne kadar vergi ödeyeceğim?

A: Nearly twenty US Dollars.
Yaklaşık yirmi Dolar.

Q: Where is the children's passport?
Çocukların pasaportları nerede?

A: The children are on this passport.
Çocuklar bu pasaporttalar.

A: OK.
Peki.

Q: I could not see your visa. Do you have visa?
Vizenizi göremiyorum. Vizeniz var mı?

A: Yes I have. Please check it on the next page.
Evet var. Lütfen diğer sayfaya bakın.

A: That is Ok. Thank you.
Her şey tamam. Teşekkürler.

Q: Will the luggage be examined now?
Bagajlar şimdi mi kontrol edilecek?

A: Yes.
Evet.

Q: Do you have anything to declare.
Deklare edeceğiniz bir şey var mı?

A: I have nothing to declare.
Hayır, hiçbir şey yok.

Q: May I close the bag?
Çantamı kapatabilir miyim?

A: Yes. Thank you.
Evet. Teşekkür ederim.

Days Months & Seasons

Günler Aylar Mevsimler

Günler

Days

Sunday	**Pazar**
Monday	**Pazartesi**
Tuesday	**Salı**
Wednesday	**Çarşamba**
Thursday	**Perşembe**
Friday	**Cuma**
Saturday	**Cumartesi**

Aylar

Months

January	**Ocak**
February	**Şubat**
March	**Mart**
April	**Nisan**
May	**Mayıs**
June	**Haziran**
July	**Temmuz**
August	**Ağustos**
September	**Eylül**
October	**Ekim**
November	**Kasım**
December	**Aralık**

Mevsimler

Seasons

winter	**kış**
spring	**ilkbahar**
summer	**yaz**
autumn / fall	**sonbahar**

Dental Problems

Diş Problemleri

abscess	**apse**
filling	**diş dolgusu**
crown	**kaplama**
dentist	**1. diş doktoru** **2. dişçi**
dentures	**1. takma diş** **2. protez**
a temporary filling	**geçici dolgu**
health insurance	**sağlık sigortası**
hurt (v.)	**1. ağrımak** **2. acımak**
pain	**ağrı**
toothache	**diş ağrısı**

Q: Is it possible to find a dentist? I have a toothache.
Bir diş doktoru bulabilir miyiz? Dişim ağrıyor.

A: Yes, there is a dentist opposite our hotel.
Evet, otelin karşısında bir doktor var.

Q: What is the problem?
Probleminiz nedir?

A: I have a toothache.
Dişim ağrıyor.

A: Ok. Please sit down and open your mouth wide.
Peki. Oturun ve ağzınızı açın.

Q: Do you feel pain now?
Şu anda ağrı hissediyor musunuz?

A: Yes. I think I have an abscess.
Evet. Sanırım apse yaptı.

A: No, not really! It needs some filling, that's all.
Hayır, apse yok. Sadece dolguya ihtiyacınız var.

Q: How many days are you going to stay here?
Burada ne kadar süre kalacaksınız?

A: We are leaving the day after tomorrow.
Yarından sonra gidiyoruz.

Q: Can you give me something for the pain?
Ağrı kesici bir şeyler verebilir misiniz?

A: I am afraid pills won't stop your pain.
Korkarım ağrınızı ilaçlar durduramaz.

A: I can do a temporary filling.
Yapabileceğim tek şey geçici dolgu.

Q: Ok. Does it hurt?
Peki. Canım yanacak mı?

A: Yes, a little.
Evet, biraz.

* * * * * *

Q: How much will it cost?
Ne kadar olabilir?

A: Fifty US Dollars.
Elli Dolar.

A: I need a receipt for my insurance.
Sigortam için bana fiş gerekli.

A: Ok. Here is your receipt.
Peki. İşte fişiniz.

A: Thank you. I feel better now.
Teşekkür ederim. Şimdi kendimi daha iyi hissediyorum.

A: Bye.
Hoşça kalın.

A: Bye.
Güle güle.

Directions
Yönler

corner	köşe
at the corner	köş**ede**
square	meydan
at the square	meydan**da**
on the left	sol**da**
on the right	sağ**da**
turn left / right	sol**a** / sağ**a** dönün
turn back	geri dönün
crossroads	kavşak
at the crossroads	kavşak**ta**
from the bank	banka**dan**
from Izmir	İzmir'**den**
nearby / close **to**	1. yakın 2. yakının**da**
next **to**	yanın**da**
next to each other	yan yana
on foot	yaya
back	1. arka 2. geri
at the back	1. arka**da** 2. geri**de**
opposite	1. ters 2. zıt 3. karşı
opposite off	1. karşı**da** 2. karşı**sında**
straight	1. doğru 2. düz
to Istanbul	İstanbul'**a**
to the museum	müze**ye**
to the station	istasyon**a**

-a, **-e** and **-dan**, **-den** are suffixes to denote a direction that corresponds to prepositions **to** and **from**. If the last syllable of the noun contains one of the front vowels: **e**, **i**, **ö**, **ü**, the suffixes **-e [to]** or **-den [from]** are used; otherwise the suffixes **-a** or **-dan** are used. It is also valid for **-da**, **-de** correspond to preposition **at**. [This rule is called Major Vowel Harmony].

Q: How do I get to Ayazma Hotel?
Ayazma Oteli'ne nasıl ulaşırım?

A: Turn back, go straight a head. It is right at the corner of the second traffic lights.
Geri dönün, doğru ilerleyin. İkinci trafik ışıklarında sağ köşededir.

Q: Is it far?
Uzak mı?

A: Not really.
Pek değil.

Q: Can I walk there?
Oraya yürüyebilir miyim.

A: Sure!
Kesinlikle!

* * * * * *

Q: Excuse me! We're looking for the Topkapi Palace.
Afedersiniz! Biz Topkapı Saray'ını arıyoruz.

A: Oh! It is far from here.
A! O buradan çok uzakta.

Q: Is this the right way to there?
Bu oraya gitmek için doğru yol mu?

A: Unfortunately not.
Ne yazık ki hayır.

Q: Can you show me on the map where we are now?
Şu anda nerede olduğumuzu haritada gösterebilir misiniz?

A: We're right here now.
Şu anda biz tam şuradayız.

A: Many thanks. I suppose we have taken the wrong way.
Çok teşekkürler. Sanırım biz yanlış yoldan gelmişiz.

Q: Hi! How do I get onto the highway?
Merhaba! Otobana nasıl çıkabiliriz?

A: Well, I hope you have a map of region.
Şey, umarım sizde bölgenin bir haritası vardır.

Q: Yes I have. Can you show me the way on the map?
Evet var. Yolu harita üzerinde gösterebilir misiniz?

A: You are here now. Turn left when you get the traffic lights.
Siz şu anda buradasınız. Trafik ışıklarına ulaşınca sola dönün.

A: The first traffic lights?
İlk ışıklarda mı?

A: Yes, that is right. And then go straight a head for about two kilometers.
Evet, doğru. Ve sonra yaklaşık iki kilometre ilerleyin.

A: Then ask someone for the exit to highway.
Sonra otobana çıkan yolu birilerine sorun.

A: Many thanks.
Çok teşekkürler.

A: Bye.
Hoşça kalın.

Diseases

Hastalıklar

allergy	**alerji**
bad cold	**1. üşütmek** **2. soğuk almak**
car sickness	**araba tutması**
constipation	**kabızlık**
cough	**öksürük**
diarrhea	**diyare**
doctor	**doktor**
fever	**ateş**
headache	**baş ağrısı**
hiccup	**hıçkırık**
insect bites	**böcek ısırması**
insomnia	**uykusuzluk**
nausea	**bulantı**
pain	**ağrı**
stomachache	**mide ağrısı**
temperature	**ateş**
tetanus	**tetanoz**
to be ill	**hasta olmak**
toothache	**diş ağrısı**

Q: I have headache. Dou you have something for the pain?
Başım ağrıyor. Ağrı kesici bir şey var mı?

A: Yes I have.
Evet var.

A: I suppose I have bad cold.
Sanırım üşüttüm.

Q: Do you have fever.
Ateşin var mı?

A: I don't know but, I don't feel well.
Bilmiyorum. Ama kendimi kötü hissediyorum.

Q: Would you like something for bad cold too?
Soğuk algınlığı (üşütme) için de bir şey ister misin?

A: I suppose I need it.
Sanırım ona ihtiyacım var.

A: Take these pills each six hours.
Bu haplardan sekiz saatte bir al.

A: I 'd like some vitamin tablets too.
Vitamine de ihtiyacım var.

Q: Would you like vitamin C pills?
C vitamini de ister misin?

A: Sure.
Elbette.

A: Take these pills two times daily with meals.
Bu hapları günde iki defa yemek aralarında iç.

Q: Do you have something for rash too?
Alerji için de bir şeylerin var mı?

A: Yes I have. Why?
Evet var. Neden?

Q: Is it safe to give it to the children?
O çocuklar için güvenli mi?

A: Oh sorry. You can not use it for children.
Ah, özür dilerim. Onu çocuklarda kullanamazsın.

Drinks

İçecekler

Soft Drinks	Alkolsüz İçecekler
a black coffee	**bir sade kahve**
a bottle of mineral water	**bir şişe mineral su**
a can of coke	**bir kutu kola**
a tea	**bir çay**
ayran * (yogurt drink)	**ayran**
coca-cola	**koka kola**
coffee	**kahve**
coffee with milk	**sütlü kahve**
coke	**kola**
for him / her	**1. onun için** **2. ona**
for me	**1. benim için** **2. bana**
for us	**1. bizim için** **2. bize**
fruit juice	**meyve suyu**
lemonade	**limonata**
low-calorie drink	**diyet içecek**
milk	**süt**
no sugar	**şekersiz**
orange-juice	**portakal suyu**
sprite	**sprite**
tea	**çay**
water / regular water	**su**
with ice	**buzlu**
with lemon	**limonlu**
with milk	**sütlü**

A: I'm very thirsty.
Çok susadım.

Q: Do you have anything non-alcoholic?
Alkolsüz içecek bir şeyleriniz var mı?

A: Sure. What will you have?
Elbette. Ne istersiniz?

Q: What would you like to drink Ann?
Ne içmek istersin Ann?

A: I'd like a cold drink. Cola with ice please.
Soğuk bir şey istiyorum. Buzlu bir kola lütfen.

Q: Would you like a drink Ahmet?
Ahmet, içecek bir şey ister misin?

A: I'd like something cold too. May I have an orange-juice?
Ben de soğuk bir şey isterim. Portakal suyu alabilir miyim?

A: Ok. A cola with ice for her, an orange-juice for him and a cup of coffee for me please.
Peki. Bayan için bir buzlu kola, bay için bir portakal suyu ve benim için bir kahve lütfen.

A: How would you like the coffee, black or white?
Kahveyi nasıl istersiniz, sade veya sütlü?

Q: A black coffee with no sugar please
Sade ve şekersiz lütfen.

A: OK. Thank you.
Peki. Teşekkür ederim.

Driving Car

Araba Kullanma

Parking is a serious problem in big cities of Turkey. I suggest all visitors to get information about parking before you intend to go any place by your car. Maybe taking a taxi will be more useful in the cities.

danger	**tehlike**
driving license	**ehliyet**
exit	**çıkış**
highway	**otoban**
lane	**şerit**
no parking	**park yapılmaz**
one-way street	**tek yönlü cadde**
road closed	**yol kapalı**
route	**1. yol** **2. güzergah**
slow down	**yavaşla**
speed limit	**hız sınırı**
stop!	**Dur!**
town centre	**şehir merkezi**
traffic lights	**1. trafik ışıkları** **2. trafik lambaları**
At The Petrol Station	
4 star	**süper benzin**
diesel	**1. mazot** **2. dizel**
petrol	**normal benzin**
unleaded	**kurşunsuz**

Q: Can I park here?
Buraya park edebilir miyim?

A: Sorry, you can't. Please go to the park over there.
Ne yazık ki hayır. Lütfen şuradaki parka gidin.

Q: Do we need a parking ticket?
Park için bilet gerekli mi?

A: Oh yes. Please pay to that person.
Ah, evet. Lütfen şu kişiye ödeyin.

Q: How long can we park for?
Ne kadar zaman park edebilirim?

A: Just for an half an hour.
Sadece yarım saat.

A: No time limit.
Zaman sınırı yok.

Q: We're going to Uludag. What's the shortest route?
Biz Uludağ'a gidiyoruz. En kestirme yol hangisidir?

A: Keep your way.
Aynı yolda devam edin.

A: Please ask someone at the first crossroad.
Lütfen ilk kavşakta birine sorun.

Q: Will there be a lot of traffic on the highway?
Otoyolda trafik yoğun olabilir mi?

A: I don't think so.
1. Sanmıyorum.
2. Sanmam.

Q: Is that pass open?
Geçit açık mıdır?

A: I don't know. Ask someone else.
Bilmiyorum. Başkasına sorun.

Q: Do we need snow chains?
Zincir gerekli mi?

A: I suppose they are necessary.
Sanırım gereklidir.

Q: Is there a petrol station near here?
Yakınlarda petrol istasyonu bulunur mu?

A: There may be one a kilometer away.
Yaklaşık bir kilometre sonra bulabilirsiniz.

Q: Can you fill this can with petrol, please?
Şu kaba benzin doldurabilir misiniz?

A: OK.
Peki.

Q: Do you take this credit card?
Bu kartı kabul ediyor musunuz?

A: Sorry, we accept only MasterCard and Visa.
Özür dilerim, sadece MasterCard ve Visa kabul ediyoruz.

A: Please check the petrol and the water.
Lütfen benzini ve suyu kontrol edin.

Q: Which pump?
Hangi pompadan istersiniz?

A: 4 star. Fill it up, please.
Süper. Depoyu doldurun lütfen.

Q: Where do I pay?
Ödemeyi nereye yapayım?

A: Go to the pay-desk please.
Gişeye yapın.

Q: Oh sorry, could you check the tire pressure too.
A pardon, lastiklerin havasını da kontrol edebilir misiniz?

A: All are OK.
Hepsi iyi durumda.

A: Back tires need some air.
Arka lastiklerin biraz havaya ihtiyacı var.

Q: Where is the air pump?
Hava pompası nerede?

Q: Where is the water?
Su nerede?

A: On the left side over there.
İleride sol tarafta.

Emergencies

Acil Durumlar

In Turkey although crime is low compared to many countries, the last reports show that it is growing because of economic crisis. So, I offer some precautions to everybody who wish to visit my country. Women appear to be the main target for muggings or robberies. As in other large metropolitan areas throughout the world, common street crimes include pick pocketing, purse-snatching, and mugging.

Service Numbers

- 155-Police
- 112-Emergency
- 110-Fire
- 118-Information

ambulance	**ambulans**
Attention please!	**Lütfen dikkat!**
casualty department	**asayiş şubesi**
doctor	**doktor**
emergency	**acil**
emergency exit	**acil çıkış**
emergency room	**acil servis**
entry	**giriş**
fire brigade	**itfaiye**
Fire!	**Yangın!**
Help!	**İmdat!**
hospital	**hastane**
pharmacy	**eczane**
police	**polis**
police station	**polis karakolu**

Q: Help! Help! Is there anyone to help me?
İmdat! İmdat! Bana yardım edecek biri var mı?

A: Please call an ambulance!
Lütfen bir ambulans çağırın!

Q: What has happened?
Ne oldu?

A: There's been an accident. Someone is injured.
Bir kaza oldu. Biri yaralandı.

Q: Please be calm! Which kind of an accident has occurred?
Lütfen sakin olun. Ne tür bir kaza oldu?

A: Someone has been knocked down by a car.
Birine bir araba çarptı.

Q: Where?
Nerede?

A: Down the street.
Caddenin aşağısında.

A: Ok. I am calling for an ambulance now.
Peki. Bir ambulans çağırıyorum.

* * * * * *

Q: Can you help me?
Yardım eder misiniz?

A: Sure.
Elbette.

Q: Where is the police station? I want to report a theft.
Polis karakolu nerede? Bir hırsızlık rapor edeceğim.

Q: What is the problem?
Problem nedir?

A: I've been robbed.
Soyuldum.

A: Please call the police!
Lütfen bir polis çağırın!

Q: Ok. I'll call now. Please tell me where has the case occurred?
Peki. Şimdi arıyorum. Lütfen olayın nerede olduğunu söyleyin.

A: I've been attacked by a young man at the corner of my hotel.
Otelimin köşesinde genç bir adam tarafından saldırıya uğradım.

Q: Are you injured?
Yaralandınız mı?

A: No. He just robbed my bag. I've lost my money and passport.
Hayır. O sadece benim çantamı kaptı. Paramı ve pasaportumu kaybettim.

Q: Hello, is it the police station? I would like to report a robbery.
Alo, polis karakolu mu? Bir soygun rapor etmek istiyorum.

A: I want to speak to a police.
Polisle konuşmak istiyorum.

Q: Ok. Would you please tell us the problem?
Peki. Lütfen problemi anlatır mısınız?

A: I have been robbed. I have lost my passport and money.
Ben soyuldum. Pasaportumu ve paramı kaybettim.

Q: Would you give me the telephone number of your hotel?
Lütfen kaldığınız otelin telefon numarasını verin.

A: I would like to phone my embassy.
Elçiliğimizi aramak istiyorum.

* * * * * *

Q: What is the matter?
Sorun neydi?

A: You went through a red light and exceeded the speed limit.
Kırmızı ışıkta geçtiniz ve hız limitini aştınız.

Q: How much is the fine?
Ceza ne kadar?

A: Nearly 50 US Dollars.
50 Dolar.

A: I didn't know there was a speed limit.
Hız limiti olduğunu bilmiyordum.

Q: Where do I pay it?
Onu nereye ödeyeceğim?

A: Sorry, you have to pay the fine now.
Özür dilerim. Cezayı şimdi ödemek zorundasınız.

Q: Do I have to pay it straightaway? I'm very sorry.
Çok özür dilerim. Hemen mi ödeyeceğim?

A: I need a report for my insurance. Please prepare a report for me.
Sigortam için bir rapor gerekli. Bir rapor hazırlar mısınız?

A: Ok. Here is your report. Please pay attention to the traffic signs.
Tamam. İşte raporunuz. Lütfen trafik işaretlerine dikkat edin.

A: I want to speak to a policewoman.
Bir bayan polisle konuşmak istiyorum.

Q: Please stop crying. What has happened?
Lütfen ağlamayın. Ne oldu?

A: I would like to phone my embassy.
Elçiliğimize telefon etmek istiyorum.

Q: Ok! Ok! Please try to tell me what has happened.
Tamam, tamam. Lütfen bana ne olduğunu anlatın.

A: I've been raped.
Tecavüze uğradım.

Q: I see. Please tell me where?
Anlıyorum. Lütfen nerede olduğunu söyleyin.

A: I would like to phone my embassy.
Elçiliğimizi aramak istiyorum.

Q: That is alright. I am calling your embassy now.
Tamam. Şimdi elçiliğinizi arıyorum.

A: Please tell them this is an urgent call.
Lütfen onlara acil olduğunu söyleyin.

Q: Ok. Ok. Do you need a doctor?
Tamam, tamam. Doktora ihtiyacınız var mı?

A: Yes please, call a doctor for me.
Evet lütfen, benim için bir doktor çağırın.

Endearment & Love Words

Sevgi Sözcükleri

Tell these words to the loved one

I love you.
Seni seviyorum.

I fell in love with you.
Sana aşık oldum.

I love you so much.
Seni çok seviyorum.

I can't live without you.
Sensiz yaşayamam.
Sensiz yapamam.

I need you.
Sana ihtiyacım var.

I need you so much.
Sana çok ihtiyacım var.

I wish you were mine.
Benim olmanı istiyorum.

I love you with all my heart.
Seni bütün kalbimle seviyorum.

Love overcomes everything.
Aşk her şeyin üstesinden gelir.

Come to me, my love.
Sevgilim, bana dön.

Love in my heart is forever.
Sevgim sonsuza kadar sürecek.

My love gets stronger day by day.
Aşkım gün geçtikçe büyüyor.

I can't live without your love.
Senin sevgin olmadan yaşayamam.

My heart is full of love.
Kalbim aşkla dolu.

Give me your love.
Bana sevgini ver.
Sevgine ihtiyacım var.

I give you all my love.
Tüm sevgimi sana veririm.

With love.
Sevgilerimle.

All I need is your love.
Tek ihtiyacım senin sevgin.

There's no happiness without your love.
Aşkın olmadan mutlu olamam.

I will always love you.
Seni her zaman seveceğim.

Let's keep our love forever.
Aşkımızı sonsuza kadar koruyalım.

I want you to know there's love in my heart.
Kalbimin aşkınla dolu olduğunu bilmeni isterim.

Our love will last forever.
Aşkımız ömür boyu sürecek.

To Send a Fax

Faks Çekmek

The country code of Turkey is **+90**. The area code of European side of Istanbul is 0 212 and Anatolian side of Istanbul is 0 216. Ankara's city code is 0 312 and Izmir's city code is 0 232. You should then dial the fax number.

Adres Address	
Kime Attention to	
Kimden From	
Tarih Date	
Konu Re:	
Sayfa sayısı Total pages	

Q: Excuse me! Do you have a fax machine?
Afedersiniz? Faks makineniz var mı?

A: Yes we have.
Evet var.

Q: I want to send a fax. Can I use your fax?
Bir faks göndermek istiyorum. Sizin faksınızı kullanabilir miyim?

A: Why not? Of course.
Neden olmasın. Tabii ki.

Q: What is your fax number?
Sizin faks numaranız kaç?

A: Our fax number is ...
Bizim faks numaramız ...

Q: I am having trouble sending the fax. Please help!
Faksımı göndermede problem yaşıyorum. Lütfen yardım edin !

A: Please retry it.
Lütfen tekrar deneyin.

Q: But I constantly get the busy signal. Would you please help me?
Fakat bu sürekli meşgul sinyali veriyor. Lütfen bana yardım eder misiniz?

A: Just a moment please. I am coming.
Bir dakika lütfen. Hemen geliyorum.

Food

Yiyecekler

Soups	**Çorbalar**
chicken soup	**tavuk suyu çorba**
lentil soup	**mercimek çorbası**
meat-broth	**et suyu**
Fast food	**Fast food**
cheese sandwich	**kaşarlı sandviç**
cheeseburger	**çizburger**
chicken sandwich	**tavuklu sandviç**
hamburger	**hamburger**
pizza	**pizza**
spaghetti	**spagetti**
Others	**Diğerleri**
beef	**dana eti**
biscuits	**bisküvi**
bread	**ekmek**
brown bread	**1. siyah ekmek** **2. kepek ekmeği**
butter	**tereyağı**
cereal	**tahıl**
cheese	**peynir**
chicken	**tavuk**
cream	**krema**
dessert	**tatlı**
egg	**yumurta**
fish	**balık**
flour	**un**
fruit	**meyva**
ham	**jambon**
honey	**bal**
ice	**buz**
ice cream	**dondurma**
jam	**reçel**
ketchup	**ketçap**
margarine	**margarin**

marmalade	**marmelat**
mayonnaise	**mayonez**
meat	**et**
milk	**süt**
mustard	**hardal**
olive oil	**zeytin yağı**
pepper	**biber**
rice	**pirinç**
salad	**salata**
salt	**tuz**
sausage	**sosis**
sugar	**şeker**
tomato	**domates**
vinegar	**sirke**
yoghurt	**yoğurt**

Fruits

Meyveler

The plant cover is really rich in Turkey. Most fruits and vegetables are natural and fresh. I suggest everybody to prefer the seasonal fresh juices which have no additives. You can find them at "**Büfe**", small places which sell fresh fruit juices, toasts, doner kebab and hamburgers.

almond	**badem**	melon	**kavun**
apple	**elma**	mulberry	**dut**
apricot	**kayısı**	nectar	**nektar**
avocado	**avokado**	oleaster	**iğde**
banana	**muz**	orange	**portakal**
bitter orange	**turunç**	peach	**şeftali**
blackberry	**böğürtlen**	pears	**armut**
cherry	**kiraz**	pineapple	**ananas**
chestnut	**kestane**	plum	**erik**
cornelian cherry	**kızılcık**	pomegranate	**nar**
fig	**incir**	quince	**ayva**
grapefruit	**greyfurt**	raspberry	**ahududu**
grapes	**üzüm**	morello / black cherry	**vişne**
hazelnut	**fındık**	strawberry	**çilek**
Japanese plum	**yenidünya**	tangerine	**mandalina**
kiwi	**kivi**	walnut	**ceviz**
lemon	**limon**	watermelon	**karpuz**
medlar	**muşmula**	wild apricot	**zerdali**

Greetings

Selamlaşma

How are you doing?	**Neler yapıyorsunuz?**
As usual.	**Her zamanki gibi.**
Bad.	**Kötüyüm.**
Bon appétit.	**Afiyet olsun.**
Bye!	**Allaha ısmarladık!** [Said by the person leaving] **Güle güle!** [Said by the person staying]
Congratulations!	**Tebrikler.**
Excuse me.	**Afedersiniz.**
Fine, thank you.	**Teşekkür ederim, iyiyim.**
Fine and you? (formal)	**Teşekkür ederim, siz nasılsınız?**
Fine and you? (informal)	**İyiyim, sen nasılsın?**
Good afternoon.	**İyi günler.**
Good bye!	**Hoşça kal!**
Good evening! (after 6 pm)	**İyi akşamlar!**
Good health to you.	**Sağlık dileklerimle.**
Good morning!	**Günaydın!**
Good night!	**İyi geceler!**
Great!	**Harika!**
Happy birthday!	**Doğum günün kutlu olsun!**
Hello! / Hi!	**Merhaba!**
How about your children? (informal)	**Çocuklardan ne haber?**
How are you doing? (formal)	**Ne yapıyorsunuz?**
How are you doing? (informal)	**1. Ne haber?** **2. Ne yapıyorsun?**
How are you? (formal)	**Nasılsınız?**
How are you? (informal)	**Nasılsın?**
How are your children? (formal)	**Çocuklarınız nasıllar?**
How do you do? (formal)	**Nasılsınız?**
I beg your pardon?	**Efendim?**
I hope to meet you again.	**Umarım tekrar görüşürüz.**
I'm pleased to meet you.	**Memnun oldum.**
I'm pleased to meet you too.	**Ben de memnun oldum.**

If God wills.	**İnşallah.**
It's a pleasure.	**Zevkle.**
Nice to see you.	**Seni gördüğüme sevindim.**
Nice to see you, too.	**Ben de.**
Not at all. / You're welcome.	**Bir şey değil.**
Not bad.	**Fena değil.**
Not so bad.	**Kötü sayılmaz.**
Not so well.	**Çok iyi değil.**
Pardon me.	**Pardon!**
Please!	**Lütfen!**
Pleased to meet you.	**Tanıştığımıza sevindim.**
See you again.	**Görüşürüz.**
See you later.	**Görüşürüz.**
See you tomorrow.	**Yarın görüşmek üzere.**
See you!	**Görüşmek üzere!**
So long.	**Görüşürüz.**
So so.	**Şöyle böyle.**
Thank You.	**1. Teşekkür ederim.** **2. Sağol.**
Thanks.	**Teşekkürler.**
Welcome.	**Hoş geldiniz.** [Said by the person inviting] **Hoş bulduk.** [Reply of the person arriving]
What's new?	**Yeni bir şey var mı?**
With my pleasures.	**Memnuniyetle.**
You are so kind.	**Çok naziksiniz.**

Health Problems

Sağlık Sorunları

Doctors and dentists: Doctors and dentists can be found in the major hospitals and in addition, there are certain foreign-operated hospitals in Istanbul.

allergy	**alerji**
bad cold	**üşütme**
blood group	**kan grubu**
diabetic	**şeker hastası**
dispensary	**dispanser**
doctor	**doktor**
headache	**baş ağrısı**
health	**sağlık**
hospital	**hastane**
insurance	**sigorta**
out-patients	**ayakta tedavi**
pain	**ağrı**
pill	**1. hap** **2. ilaç**
pregnant	**hamile**
receipt	**1. fiş** **2. makbuz**
surgery	**ameliyat**
temperature	**ateş**
to be ill	**hasta olmak**
x-ray	**röntgen**

Q: I need a doctor. My son is ill.
Bir doktora ihtiyacımız var. Oğlum hastalandı.

Q: Really! What is the problem?
Gerçekten mi? Neyi var?

A: He has a high temperature.
Ateşi yüksek.

Q: Will he have to go to the hospital?
Hastaneye gitmesi gerekir mi?

A: I suppose yes. Please call a taxi for us.
Sanırım evet. Lütfen bizim için bir taksi çağırın.

A: Ok. I call a taxi.
Peki. Hemen bir taksi çağırıyorum.

* * * * * *

A: I have a pain here.
Buram ağrıyor.

Q: Ok. I'll have a look now. Do you feel any pain here?
Peki. Şimdi bir bakalım. Şurası ağrıyor mu?

A: Yes and here.
Evet ve şurası.

A: Don't worry, there is no serious problem. He has caught a cold.
Merak etmeyin, önemli bir problem yok. Sadece biraz üşütmüş.

Q: Ok. Many thanks. Any medicine needed?
Peki çok teşekkürler. İlaç verecek misiniz?

A: I will write a prescription. Please buy these from a pharmacy.
Reçete yazacağım. Lütfen bu ilaçları bir eczaneden alın.

Q: Will I have to pay? How much does it cost?
Bir şey ödeyecek miyim? Ne kadar?

A: A hundred Lira.
Yüz Lira lütfen.

Q: May I have a receipt for my insurance?
Sağlık sigortam için bir fiş alabilir miyim?

A: Ok. Here you are. I am sure he will get well soon.
Peki. İşte fişiniz. Kısa zamanda iyileşeceğinden eminim.

A: Many thanks. Bye.
Çok teşekkürler. Hoşça kalın.

Hobbies & Interests

Hobiler ve İlgi Alanları

belly dance	**oryantal**
belly dancer (female)	**dansöz**
collecting	**koleksiyonculuk**
cycling	**bisiklet sporu**
dancer	**dansçı**
diving	**1. dalış** **2. dalgıçlık**
fishing	**balıkçılık**
football	**futbol**
jogging	**yavaş koşu**
listen (v.)	**dinlemek**
match	**maç**
music	**müzik**
painting	**resim yapmak**
play (v.)	**1. çalmak** (for instruments) **2. oynamak** (for games)
reading	**okumak**
ride (v.) (bicycle, horse)	**binmek**
running	**koşu**
swimming	**yüzme**
tennis	**tenis**
tennis court	**tenis kortu**
volleyball	**voleybol**

Q: We'd like to go to a belly dance show.
Biz oryantal dans gösterisine gitmek istiyoruz.

A: Really! There are some night clubs near by Taksim.
Öyle mi! Taksim civarında bazı gece kulüpleri var.

Q: Is reservation needed?
Rezervasyon gerekli mi?

A: Yes it is. I know a good place.
Evet gerekli. Ben güzel bir yer biliyorum.

Q: Is there a good dancer?
İyi dansöz var mı?

A: Yes. She is quite a good dancer.
Evet. O oldukça iyi bir dansöz.

Q: How can we make a reservation?
Nasıl rezervasyon yaptırabiliriz?

A: I can help you to make a reservation.
Ben size yardım edebilirim.

A: Many thanks. Please make a reservation for six people.
Teşekkürler. Lütfen altı kişilik rezervasyon yaptırın.

Q: What do you do in your spare times?
Boş zamanlarında ne yaparsın?

A: I generally listen to music. Music is a hobby of mine.
Genellikle müzik dinlerim. Müzik benim hobimdir.

Q: Really. Do you play an instrument?
Gerçekten mi? Bir enstrüman çalıyor musun?

A: Yes, I play guitar.
Evet, gitar çalıyorum.

A: I like watching football matches.
Ben futbol maçı seyretmekten hoşlanırım.

Q: Which is your favorite team?
Favori takımın hangisi?

A: Galatasaray is my favorite.
Galatasaray benim favori takımımdır.

Q: Do you also like playing football?
Futbol oynamaktan da hoşlanır mısın?

A: Not really. I like just watching but, I like playing table tennis.
Pek değil. Ben sadece seyretmeyi severim, fakat masa tenisi oynamayı severim.

A: I like photography. I also like playing tennis.
Ben fotoğraf çekmekten hoşlanırım. Aynı zamanda tenis oynamaktan da hoşlanırım.

Q: Would you like to play tennis with me?
Benimle tenis oynamak ister misin?

A: Why not! We can play this afternoon if you like.
Neden olmasın! İstersen bu akşamüstü oynayalım.

* * * * * *

Q: What are your hobbies?
Hobilerin nelerdir?

Q: My favorite hobby is gardening. What is yours?
Benim favori hobim bahçeciliktir. Seninkiler nedir?

A: I like fishing.
Ben balık avlamaktan hoşlanırım.

Q: Other interests?
Başka ilgi alanın?

A: Oh, I like cycling. How about yours?
Ah, bisiklete binmekten hoşlanırım, ya sen?

A: I like cycling too.
Bisiklete binmeyi ben de severim.

Q: Would you like to race with me?
Benimle yarışmak ister misin?

A: Why not! That is Ok.
Neden olmasın! Tamam.

Q: Where can we hire bikes?
Nereden bisiklet kiralayabiliriz?

A: I am going to ask for the receptionist.
Resepsiyon memuruna soracağım.

Q: Is there any shop that hires bikes?
Buralarda bisiklet kiralayan bir dükkan var mı?

A: There must be one next to the post office.
Postanenin yanında bir tane olmalı.

Q: How much would it be per hour?
Saati kaç Liradır?

A: I don't know exactly. But, I can call them if you like.
Kesin olarak bilmiyorum. Fakat, isterseniz telefon ederim.

A: Yes please, ask for me the prices.
Evet lütfen, fiyatı benim için öğrenin.

In a Hotel

Otelde

a room	**bir oda**
bathroom	**banyo**
bed	**yatak**
bed and breakfast	**oda - kahvaltı**
hotel	**otel**
No vacancies.	**Boş yer yok.**
reservation	**rezervasyon**
room	**oda**
room service	**oda servisi**
Rooms available.	**Boş oda bulunur.**
shower	**duş**
two people	**iki kişi**
Where is the toilet? Where is the restroom?	**Tuvalet nerede?**

Q: Hello! Do you have a list of accommodation with prices?
Merhaba! Kalınabilecek yerler ve fiyatlarını içeren bir listeniz var mı?

A: Yes, here you are.
Evet, işte buyrun.

A: Sorry, we haven't.
Özür dilerim yok.

Q: Is there a hotel around here?
Buralarda hiç otel var mı?

Q: Do you know a good place to stay for tonight?
Bu gece için kalacak iyi bir yer biliyor musunuz?

Q: Are there any vacancies for tonight?
Bu akşam için hiç boş yeriniz var mı?

Q: Are there any vacancies?
Hiç boş yeriniz var mı?

Q: Do you have a room for tonight?
Bu akşam için bir odanız var mı?

Q: Do you have any vacancies?
Boş odanız var mı?

A: Yes, would you like to see?
Evet, görmek ister misiniz?

Q: Yes please. Do you have a lift?
Evet lütfen. Asansörünüz var mı?

A: Unfortunately not.
Ne yazık ki yok.

A: This is the room!
İşte odanız!

A: I think it is too small. Do you have another one?
Sanırım bu çok küçük. Başka var mı?

Q: Would you like a room on the ground floor?
Giriş katında bir oda ister misiniz?

A: Why not! If it is bigger one... Yes.
Neden olmasın! Eğer daha büyükse... Evet.

Internal Body Parts

İç Organlar

appendicitis	**apandisit**
belly	**göbek**
blood	**kan**
bone	**kemik**
brain	**beyin**
gall bladder	**safra kesesi**
heart	**kalp**
intestine	**bağırsak**
kidney	**böbrek**
liver	**karaciğer**
lung	**akciğer**
muscle	**kas**
pancreas	**pankreas**
skeleton	**iskelet**
skin	**deri**
spleen	**dalak**
stomach	**mide**
vein	**damar**

Language Names

Diller

Language names are formed by the suffixes **-ce** or **-ca** added to the nationality names. Another point is the suffixes **-ce** or **-ca** become **-çe** or **-ça** if the last consonant of the nationality name has one of these letters:
ç, f, h, k, p, s, ş, t.

Albanian	**Arnavutça**	Korean	**Korece**
Arabic	**Arapça**	Kurdish	**Kürtçe**
Armenian	**Ermenice**	Latin	**Latince**
Azerbaijani	**Azerice**	Macedonian	**Makedonca**
Bulgarian	**Bulgarca**	Mayan	**Mayaca**
Catalan	**Katalanca**	Norwegian	**Norveççe**
Chinese	**Çince**	Portuguese	**Portekizce**
Czech	**Çekçe**	Romanian	**Romence**
Danish	**Danimarkaca**	Russian	**Rusça**
Dutch	**Hollandaca**	Scottish	**İskoçça**
English	**İngilizce**	Serbian	**Sırpça**
Finnish	**Fince**	Slovak	**Slovakça**
French	**Fransızca**	Slovenian	**Slovence**
German	**Almanca**	Spanish	**İspanyolca**
Greek	**Yunanca**	Swedish	**İsveççe**
Hindi	**Hintçe**	Tajik	**Tacikçe**
Hungarian	**Macarca**	Tatar	**Tatarca**
Irish	**İrlandaca**	Turkish	**Türkçe**
Italian	**İtalyanca**	Turkmen	**Türkmence**
Japanese	**Japonca**	Uighur	**Uygurca**
Kazakh	**Kazakça**	Uzbek	**Özbekçe**
Kirghiz / Kyrgyz	**Kırgızca**	Vietnamese	**Vietnamca**

Laundry

Çamaşır Yıkama

Doing the washing may be a problem for tourists because not many laundries are available for public use. Each house has its own washing machine as a consequence of the marketing policy of companies who produce these machines. Besides all big hotels and also some small hotels have laundry services. There are also a couple of laundries in localized tourism areas. Please check if it has a laundry service before you book your hotel. Otherwise you have to do it yourself by hand in an old fashion way! Dry cleaners are also available anywhere except some really small towns.

dry - cleaning	**kuru temizleme**
drying machine	**kurutma makinesi**
iron	**ütü**
launderette	**çamaşırhane**
laundry	**1. çamaşır** **2. çamaşırhane**
washing machine	**çamaşır makinesi**
washing powder	**deterjan**

Q: Do you have dry - cleaning service?
Kuru temizleme servisiniz var mı?

A: Unfortunately we haven't.
Ne yazık ki yok.

Q: So, where can I do some washing?
Öyleyse, çamaşırlarımı nerede yıkayabilirim?

A: There are only two launderette services in this town.
Bu kasabada sadece iki çamaşırhane var.

Q: Where is the nearest launderette?
En yakın çamaşırhane nerede?

A: One of them is very close to us.
Bir tanesi bize çok yakın.

Q: Can I have my laundry washed here?
Çamaşırlarımı burada yıkatabilir miyim?

A: Sorry, we can't do it for you. But, you can do it by yourself.
Özür dilerim biz yapamıyoruz. Fakat kendiniz yapabilirsiniz.

Q: What coins do I need?
Hangi bozuk para gerekli?

A: Please get some token from the cashier up there.
Lütfen kasadan jeton satın alın.

Q: Is there somewhere I can dry my clothes?
Çamaşırlarımı kurutabileceğim bir yer var mı?

A: Yes there is a drying machine up there.
Evet şurada bir kurutma makinesi var.

Q: Can you iron this for me?
Bunları ütüleyebilir misiniz?

A: Sorry madam, this is a self service launderette.
Özür dilerim bayan, burası self-servis bir çamaşırhanedir.

Q: Ok. Can I borrow an iron?
Peki. Bir ütü ödünç alabilir miyim?

A: Please ask that young lady.
Lütfen şu genç bayandan isteyin.

* * * * * *

Q: Hello, the room service?
Alo, oda servisi mi?

A: Please, come to collect my clothes to be washed.
Lütfen giyeceklerimi yıkanması için gelip alın.

Q: When will my things be ready?
Eşyalarım ne zaman hazır olur?

A: All will be ready in this afternoon madam.
Hepsi öğleden sonra hazır olur bayan.

Q: Ok. Do you need a list?
Peki. Bir liste vereyim mi?

A: Yes please.
Evet lütfen.

Q: Here is the list. Will it be ready until two o'clock?
İşte liste. Saat ikiye kadar hazır olur mu?

A: Sure.
Kesinlikle.

A: Thank you.
Teşekkür ederim.

Luggage

Bagaj

You often need to pay 5 to 10 YTL (New Turkish Lira-nearly 2 to 5 US Dollars) to porters who help to carry your luggage, so make sure you have some change on arrival.

baggage	**bagaj**
baggage claim	**bagaj gelişi**
closed	**kapalı**
collect (v.)	**1. almak** **2. toplamak**
leave (v.)	**1. bırakmak** **2. terk etmek**
left - luggage locker	**bagaj saklama dolabı**
left - luggage office	**emanet**
open	**açık**
reclaim (v.)	**geri almak**
rucksack	**sırt çantası**
send (v.)	**göndermek**
suitcase	**bavul**
what	**ne**
where	**nerede**

Q: My luggage isn't there. Where can I find my luggage?
Benim bagajlarım orada yok. Onları nerede bulabilirim?

A: Please check it again carefully.
Lütfen dikkatlice tekrar kontrol edin.

Q: What has happened to the luggage on the flight from Bern?
Bern uçağının bagajlarına ne oldu?

Q: What is the matter?
Problem nedir?

A: My suitcase has been damaged on the flight.
Bavulum uçakta hasar görmüş.

A: Please go to the complaints department.
Lütfen şikayet bürosuna başvurun.

Q: Can you help me with my luggage, please?
Bagajlarıma yardım edebilir misiniz?

A: Certainly madam.
Elbette bayan.

Q: When does the left luggage office open and close?
Emanetin açılış kapanış saatleri ne zaman?

A: I don't know madam.
Ben bilmiyorum, bayan.

Q: Excuse me! May I leave it here until 6 o'clock?
Afedersiniz! Onu saat altıya kadar bırakabilir miyim?

A: Sure.
Elbette.

A: Can I leave this overnight?
Bunu gece boyunca bırakabilir miyim?

A: Don't worry; we serve 7 days 24 hours.
Merak etmeyin biz 24 saat açığız.

A: I'll take it at eight thirty am tomorrow morning. Ok?
Onu yarın sabah sekiz buçukta alırım. Tamam mı?

A: OK. Thank you.
Tamam. Teşekkürler.

* * * * * *

A: Please, take my luggage to the room.
Bagajlarımı odaya götürün lütfen.

Q: Where is your luggage?
Bagajlarınız nerede?

A: My luggage is in the car.
Bagajlarım arabada.

Q: Where is your luggage Robert?
Robert senin bagajların nerede?

Q: Is this your luggage?
Bu sizin bagajınız mı?

A: Yes it is. Be careful with this suitcase please.
Evet. Şu bavula dikkat edin lütfen.

Q: Is everything Ok with your luggage?
Bagajlarınız tamam mı?

A: My briefcase has disappeared from the room number 201.
Benim evrak çantam iki yüz bir (201) numaralı odadan yok oldu.

Q: Really! How many briefcases do you have?
Gerçekten mi! Sizin kaç tane evrak çantanız var?

A: Just one.
Sadece bir tane.

A: You are holding one on your left hand!
Sol elinizde bir tane var!

A: Oh, I am terribly sorry. Thanks.
Oh, çok özür dilerim. Teşekkürler.

Marriage Proposal

Evlenme Teklifi

Tell these words to your lady to marry you

Will you marry me?
Benimle evlenir misin?

I want you to be my wife.
Benim karım olmanı istiyorum.

Let's get married.
Haydi evlenelim.

I love you very much and would like to ask you to be my wife.
Seni çok seviyorum ve karım olmanı istiyorum.

All I dream about is the day you will be my wife.
Tek hayalim benim karım olman.

All I pray to God is you saying "Yes!"
Allah'tan tek dileğim bana "Evet!" demen.

Be my wife!
Karım ol!

Marry me!
Evlen benimle!

We are created for each other. Say "Yes!"
Biz birbirimiz için yaratılmışız. Lütfen "Evet!" de.

I dream about the day when we'll be a family.
Aile olacağımız günü hayal ediyorum.

We feel so good together. Let's make a family.
Birbirimizle çok mutluyuz. Haydi bir aile kuralım.

I want so badly we had a real family.
Gerçek bir aile kurmamızı çok istiyorum.

Let's create a real family.
Haydi gerçek bir aile kuralım.

I want you so much to marry me.
Benimle evlenmeni çok istiyorum.

Please be my wife!
Lütfen karım ol!

Finally I want to tell you this: Would you be my wife!
Sonunda bunu söyleyeceğim: Karım olur musun?

Measures & Quantities

Ölçüler ve Miktarlar

International numeric system was introduced in 1928 and the metric system was introduced in 1931 in Turkey.

To have some idea about **Ataturk's Revolutions** please visit **http://www.kulturturizm.gov.tr/portal/tarih_en.asp?belgeno=5244**.

250 grams of grapes	**250 gram üzüm**
a bottle of Coca-Cola	**bir şişe Coca-Cola**
a dozen of pencils	**bir düzine kalem**
a glass of water	**bir bardak su**
a jar of jam	**bir kavanoz reçel**
a kilo of apple	**bir kilo elma**
a large glass	**büyük bardak**
a liter of milk	**bir litre süt**
a pack of cigarette	**bir paket sigara**
a portion of salad	**bir porsiyon salata**
a quarter	**çeyrek**
a slice of bread	**bir dilim ekmek**
a small glass	**küçük bardak**
a third	**üçte bir**
a tin of beer	**bir kutu bira**
enough	**yeter**
less	**daha az**
more	**1. daha fazla** **2. daha çok**
percent	**yüzde**

Medicine

İlaçlar

antiacid tablets	**antiasit tablet**
antibiotic	**antibiyotik**
antiseptic	**antiseptik**
Aspirin	**Aspirin**
bandage	**bandaj**
chemist's (UK) pharmacy (US)	**eczane**
cold	**soğuk**
cold tablets	**soğuk algınlığı tableti**
condoms	**kondom**
cotton wool	**pamuk**
cough drops	**öksürük damlası**
disinfectant	**dezenfektan**
dose	**doz**
drugstore	**drugstore**
dry skin lotion	**nemlendirici**
duty chemist	**eczacı**
external use	**harici kullanım**
eye drops	**göz damlası**
first - aid box	**ilk yardım çantası**
injection	**enjeksiyon**
internal use	**ağızdan kullanım**
laxative	**laksatif**
medicine	**ilaç**
night service chemist's	**nöbetçi eczane**
pharmacy	**eczane**
pill	**hap**
plasters	**plaster**
prescription	**reçete**
sanitary pads	**ped**
sedative	**sakinleştirici**
skin cream	**cilt kremi**
sleeping pills	**uyku ilacı**
sunburn	**güneş yanığı**

sunburn spray	**güneş yanığı spreyi**
suppository	**supozituvar**
syrup	**şurup**
tampons	**tampon**
thermometer	**termometre**
toothbrush	**diş fırçası**
vaccine	**aşı**
vitamins	**vitamin**

Money

Para

Turkish Lira:

Attention please!
The Turkish Lira has been converted starting 01 January 2005. The national monetary unit was the Turkish Lira (TL). The amounts were in 50,000, 100,000 and 250,000 Lira denominations. Bank notes were of 500,000, 1,000,000, 5,000,000, 10,000,000, and 20,000,000 Liras.
The new currency unit of the Republic of Turkey is the New Turkish Lira. One million Turkish Lira (1.000.000 TL) is equivalent to one New Turkish Lira (1 NTL). In other words, 6 zeros has been dropped from our currency. The sub-unit of New Turkish Lira is "New Kuruş". One New Turkish Lira (NTL) is equivalent to a hundred New Kuruş (NKr). Current banknotes and coins will be in circulation until the end of 2005.

Exchange offices in tourist areas are generally open until midnight and the exchange rates for foreign currencies are published daily. All major credit cards are accepted.

Exchange Services and Rates:
You can exchange major currencies in two ways. You can use banks or exchange offices **(DÖVİZ BÜROSU)**, both of which can be found in the city center. Choosing these exchange companies will be profitable than the banks. Exchange offices are open for longer hours than banks and do not charge commission. Many are also open on Saturdays.

Cash Dispensers:
Cash dispensers (ATM - Automatic Teller Machines) usually do not let you choose which language to carry out the transaction in. Also, in smaller places, you might have trouble finding the one that takes your card.

bank notes	**kağıt para**
cashier	**kasiyer**
change	**değiştirmek**
closed	**kapalı**
Dollar	**Dolar**
exchange	**döviz bozdurmak**
list of rates of exchange	**döviz kurları**

money changing window	**para değiştirme gişesi**
note	**kağıt para**
open	**açık**
payment	**ödeme**
Pound	**Sterlin**
small change	**bozuk para**
pay (v.)	**ödemek**
tourist check	**turist çeki**
traveler's checks	**seyahat çeki**
where	**nerede**

Q: Where can I change some money?
Nerede döviz bozdurabilirim?

A: There is a foreign exchange office next to the book seller.
Kitapçının yanında bir döviz bürosu var.

Q: Shall I have to wait long?
Çok bekleyecek miyim?

A: I am busy now. Please go to the next window.
Şu anda ben meşgulüm. Yandaki gişeye gidin lütfen.

Q: Can you change these notes into Turkish Liras?
Bu paraları Türk Lirasına çevirebilir misiniz?

A: Give them to me please.
Onları bana verin lütfen.

Q: What rate do you have now?
Kurunuz ne kadar?

A: Please check it from the list on the wall.
Duvardaki listeden kontrol edin lütfen.

A: That is Ok. Please give me small notes.
Tamam. Lütfen bana bozuk para verin.

Q: Do you change traveler's checks?
Seyahat çeki bozuyor musunuz?

A: Sorry. We can't accept traveler's checks. Go to a bank immediately.
Özür dilerim. Biz seyahat çeki kabul etmiyoruz. Hemen bir bankaya gidin.

Q: When do the banks close?
Bankalar ne zaman kapanır?

A: At five pm. They are closing soon.
Saat beşte. Onlar kapanmak üzere.

Numbers

Sayılar

1	- bir	22	- yirmi iki
2	- iki	23	- yirmi üç
3	- üç	24	- yirmi dört
4	- dört	25	- yirmi beş
5	- beş	26	- yirmi altı
6	- altı	27	- yirmi yedi
7	- yedi	28	- yirmi sekiz
8	- sekiz	29	- yirmi dokuz
9	- dokuz	30	- otuz
10	- on	40	- kırk
11	- on bir	50	- elli
12	- on iki	60	- altmış
13	- on üç	70	- yetmiş
14	- on dört	80	- seksen
15	- on beş	90	- doksan
16	- on altı	100	- yüz
17	- on yedi	200	- iki yüz
18	- on sekiz	300	- üç yüz
19	- on dokuz	1000	- bin
20	- yirmi	1001	- bin bir
21	- yirmi bir	1100	- bin yüz
		2000	- iki bin

Occupations & Jobs

Meslekler ve İşler

accountant	**1. muhasebeci** **2. sayman**
actor	**aktör**
actress	**aktris**
announcer	**spiker**
archaeologist	**arkeolog**
architect	**mimar**
astronaut	**astronot**
athlete	**atlet**
auctioneer	**1. mezatçı** **2. açık artırmacı**
auditor	**1. denetçi** **2. murakıp**
author	**yazar**
baby - sitter	**çocuk bakıcısı**
baker	**fırıncı**
barman	**barmen**
barrister (court)	**avukat**
beautician	**güzellik uzmanı**
bookkeeper	**1. sayman** **2. muhasebeci**
botanist	**botanikçi**
builder	**inşaatçı**
butcher	**kasap**
carpenter	**marangoz**
cartoonist	**karikatürist**
cashier	**kasiyer**
chef	**aşçıbaşı**
clerk	**sekreter**
composer	**1. besteci** **2. kompozitor**
conductor	**1. biletçi** **2. kondüktör**
confectioner	**şekerlemeci**

cook	**aşçı**
counselor	**danışman**
dancer	**dansçı**
dentist	**1. diş doktoru** **2. dişçi**
director (company)	**1. müdür** **2. yönetici**
doctor	**doktor**
driver	**sürücü**
economist	**iktisatçı**
electrician	**elektrikçi**
engineer	**mühendis**
farmer	**çiftçi**
fireman	**itfaiyeci**
fisherman	**balıkçı**
fishmonger	**1. balık satıcısı** **2. balıkçı**
florist	**çiçekçi**
footballer	**futbolcu**
golfer	**golfçü**
greengrocer	**manav**
grocer	**bakkal**
guide	**rehber**
hairdresser	**kuaför**
headmaster	**okul müdürü**
historian	**tarihçi**
house painter	**1. badanacı** **2. boyacı**
instructor	**eğitmen**
intern	**1. stajyer** **2. stajyer doktor**
interpreter	**tercüman**
ironmonger	**hırdavatçı**
jeweler	**kuyumcu**
journalist	**gazeteci**
judge	**1. yargıç** **2. hakem**

landscaper	**peyzaj tasarımcısı**
lawyer / attorney	**avukat**
lifeguard	**cankurtaran**
machinist	**makinist**
manager	**1. yönetici** **2. müdür**
manicurist	**manikürcü**
manufacturer	**1. fabrikatör** **2. imalatçı**
mathematician	**matematikçi**
mechanic	**tamirci**
milkman	**sütçü**
miner	**maden işçisi**
movie star	**film yıldızı**
musician	**müzisyen**
nurse	**hemşire**
official	**memur**
operator (telephone)	**santral memuru**
optician	**1. gözlükçü** **2. optisyen**
orator	**1. konuşmacı** **2. hatip**
pediatrician	**çocuk doktoru**
painter	**ressam**
park ranger	**park bekçisi**
pharmacist	**eczacı**
photographer	**fotoğrafçı**
physicist	**fizikçi**
pianist	**piyanist**
pilot	**pilot**
policeman	**polis**
politician	**politikacı**
postman	**postacı**
priest	**papaz**
printer	**matbaacı**
programmer	**bilgisayar programcısı**
psychiatrist	**psikiyatrist**

psychologist	**psikolog**
psychotherapist	**psikoterapist**
publisher	**1. yayımcı** **2. yayınevi**
receptionist	**resepsiyon memuru**
reporter	**muhabir**
sailor	**denizci**
salesclerk	**tezgahtar**
scientist	**bilim adamı**
sculptor	**heykeltıraş**
secretary	**sekreter**
security guard	**güvenlik**
singer	**şarkıcı**
soldier	**asker**
songwriter	**şarkı yazarı**
stationer	**kırtasiyeci**
statistician	**istatistikçi**
stockbroker	**borsacı**
supervisor	**1. müfettiş** **2. danışman**
surgeon	**cerrah**
tailor	**terzi**
taxi driver	**taksi şoförü**
teacher	**öğretmen**
technician	**teknisyen**
tour guide	**tur rehberi**
translator	**çevirmen**
travel agent	**seyahat acentesi**
typist	**daktilo memuru**
waiter	**garson**
writer	**yazar**

Office

İş Yeri

The term office **(ofis)** is used in Turkish too but, **(iş yeri)** is the most common Turkish term used in daily life.

appointment	**randevu**
cell phone	**cep telefonu**
division	**bölüm**
document	**1. belge** **2. evrak**
extension	**1. dahili numara** **2. dahili hat**
fax	**faks**
file	**dosya**
folder	**klasör**
invoice	**fatura**
no smoking	**sigara içilmez**
notebook	**defter**
office building	**işyeri binası**
papers	**evrak**
photocopy	**fotokopi**
printer	**yazıcı**
reception (desk)	**1. resepsiyon** **2. kabul**
sales manager	**satış müdürü**
secretary	**sekreter**
shelf	**raf**
switchboard	**telefon santralı**
waste paper basket	**atık kağıt sepeti**

Q: Hello, who is speaking?
Merhaba, kimsiniz?

A: Hello. This is Kemal Aydın. I'd like to speak to Ahmet Celik.
Merhaba. Ben Kemal Aydın. Ahmet Çelik ile görüşmek istiyorum.

Q: Sorry he is not in. Would you like to leave a message?
Özür dilerim, şu anda burada değil. Not bırakmak ister misiniz?

A: I'd like to make an appointment with him.
Ondan randevu alacaktım.

Q: 10:30 am on Tuesday. Is that Ok?
Salı günü saat 10:30 da. Sizce de uygun mu?

A: That is OK. Thank you.
Tamam. Teşekkürler.

Q: Please give me your address.
Lütfen adresinizi verin.

A: Istiklal Street 3 / 1 (three slash one) Taksim.
İstiklal Caddesi, üç taksim bir, Taksim.

Q: Which floor?
Kaçıncı kat?

A: Third floor.
Üçüncü kat.

A: Thank you. Bye
Teşekkür ederim. Hoşça kalın.

A: You are welcome. Bye.
Bir şey değil. Güle güle.

* * * * * *

A: Hello. This is Kemal Aydin.
Merhaba ben Kemal Aydın.

A: Welcome Mr. Aydin. Mr. Ahmet Celik is waiting for you.
Hoş geldiniz. Ahmet Bey sizi bekliyor.

A: Do come in please!
İçeri girin lütfen!

A: Hello, this is Kemal Aydin.
Merhaba. Ben Kemal Aydın.

Q: How do you do? Take a seat please.
Nasılsınız? Bir sandalye çekin lütfen.

A: Thanks for your time.
Bana zaman ayırdığınız için çok teşekkür ederim.

Q: Unfortunately, I have only a few moments.
Maalesef sizinle birkaç dakika görüşebilirim.

A: No problem at all. I would like to introduce to you my company.
Önemli değil. Size firmamı tanıtmak istiyorum.

Q: Ok. Do you use a courier service?
Peki. Kurye servisiniz var mı?

A: Yes we have one. I wish to discuss our opportunity with really cheap prices.
Evet var. Sizinle gerçekten çok ucuz olan fiyatlarımızı konuşmak istiyorum.

Q: Would you mind if I ask you cut short?
Biraz kısa kesmenizi rica edebilir miyim?

A: That is Ok. I wish I had a price list to send you. It is a pity I have forgotten to take one when I left my office.
Sorun değil. Size fiyat listemizi göndermek isterdim. Ne yazık ki işyerimden çıkarken yanıma almayı unutmuşum.

Q: Can you send your price list via fax or e-mail to me?
Fiyat listenizi faks ya da e-mail ile gönderebilir misiniz?

A: Yes I can. I can fax it to you tomorrow morning.
Evet yaparım. Size yarın sabah fakslarım.

Q: Thank you. I'll take it in my consideration if your prices are cheaper than the company we are dealing with. Ok?
Teşekkür ederim. Fiyatlarınız halen çalıştığımız firmadan daha ucuzsa dikkate alacağım. Tamam mı?

A: That is Ok. I do not want to keep you busy. Many thanks.
Tamam. Sizi daha çok meşgul etmek istemem. Çok teşekkürler.

A: You are welcome. I hope to hear from you soon.
Bir şey değil. Umarım yakında görüşürüz.

A: Thanks a lot. Bye.
Çok teşekkürler. İyi günler.

Payment

Ödeme Yapmak

amount	**1. tutar** **2. miktar**
bill	**fatura**
by check	**çekle**
by credit card	**kredi kartıyla**
cash desk	**ödeme gişesi**
cash price	**peşin para**
discount	**1. indirim** **2. iskonto**
How much?	**Ne kadar?**
in advance	**peşin**
put on	**1. eklemek** **2. ilave etmek**
receipt	**1. makbuz** **2. fatura**
sale	**indirimli satış**
accept (v.)	**kabul etmek**
pay (v.)	**ödemek**
VAT	**1. KDV** **2. katma değer vergisi**

Q: May I have the bill, please?
Faturamı rica edebilir miyim lütfen?

A: Just a moment madam.
Bir dakika bayan.

A: Excuse me! I'm still waiting for the bill.
Afedersiniz! Hala faturamı bekliyorum.

Q: Pardon!
Pardon!

A: Yes madam!
Evet bayan!

Q: I think you made a mistake. Would you please check this bill?
Sanırım bir hata yaptınız. Şu faturayı kontrol eder misiniz?

A: The amount to be paid in is 25 Turkish Liras. What is the problem?
Ödemeniz gereken toplam tutar 25 TL. Problem nedir?

Q: How much is the lemonade?
Limonata ne kadar?

A: It is fifty Kurus.
Elli Kuruş.

A: Oops! Sorry you are right. I am going to have the sum corrected.
Ah! Haklısınız. Toplamı düzelttirmeye gidiyorum.

Q: Could you bring me the bill?
Faturayı getirir misiniz?

A: Here you are your bill, madam.
İşte faturanız efendim.

Q: Is service included?
Servis dahil mi?

A: No madam.
Hayır bayan.

A: Put it on my bill please.
Onu da faturaya ekleyin lütfen.

A: Ok. I put it on.
Peki. Ekledim.

Q: Do you accept credit card?
Kredi kartı kabul ediyor musunuz?

A: Sure.
Elbette.

A: Thanks.
Teşekkürler.

* * * * * *

Q: How much is it?
O ne kadar?

A: Two and a half Lira Sir.
İki buçuk Lira Bayım.

A: Ok. I'll buy it.
Peki. Bunu alıyorum.

Q: Please pay to the cashier.
Lütfen kasiyere ödeyin.

Q: Could I have a receipt, please?
Fiş alabilir miydim?

A: Here you are.
Buyrun.

Q: Is VAT included?
KDV dahil mi?

A: Sure.
Elbette.

Q: Do you take checks?
Çek alır mısınız?

A: Sorry we accept only credit cards.
Özür dilerim. Biz sadece kredi kartı kabul ediyoruz.

Q: Is there any discount for cash price.
Peşin ödemeye bir indirim var mı?

A: Yes a 5 % discount is available.
Evet % 5 (yüzde beş) indirim yapılabilir.

A: I'd like to pay it in advance?
Peşin ödemek istiyorum.

Q: Do you have some small changes?
Bozuk paranız var mı?

Q: I've nothing smaller.
Hiç bozuğum yok.

A: Ok. No problem at all. Here you are your change.
Peki. Önemli değil. Paranızın üstünü alın.

Petrol Station

Benzinci / Petrol İstasyonu

4 star	**süper benzin**
air	**hava**
battery	**akü**
check (v.)	**kontrol etmek**
diesel	**1. mazot** **2. dizel**
fill (v.)	**doldurmak**
flat tire	**patlak lastik**
oil	**yağ**
petrol	**normal benzin**
petrol station	**1. petrol istasyonu** **2. benzinci**
pressure	**basınç**
pump	**pompa**
radiator	**radyatör**
tank	**depo**
tire	**dış lastik**
tire pressure	**lastik havası**
unleaded	**kurşunsuz**
water	**su**

A: Is there a petrol station around here?
Buralarda bir benzinci var mı?

A: Hello. The tank is nearly empty. Fill it up, please.
Merhaba. Depo neredeyse boş. Lütfen doldurun.

Q: Which pump?
Hangi pompa?

A: Put in 40 liters of unleaded petrol.
40 litre kurşunsuz benzin koyun.

A: Please, check the oil level too.
Lütfen, yağ seviyesini de kontrol edin.

Q: One more request. Can you check the tire pressure?
Bir ricam daha var. Lastikleri de kontrol edebilir misiniz?

A: Your front tires need some air Sir.
Ön lastiklerinizin havaya ihtiyacı var beyefendi.

Q: Where is the air line?
Hava pompası nerede?

A: Up there.
Şurada.

Q: Where do I pay?
Ödemeyi nereye yapacağım?

A: Please go to the pay office on the right.
Lütfen sağdaki gişeye gidin.

Q: Do you take this credit card?
Bu kredi kartını kabul ediyor musunuz?

A: Yes Sir.
Evet beyefendi.

A: Thank you Sir. Have a good trip.
Teşekkürler beyefendi. İyi yolculuklar.

A: Thanks.
Teşekkürler.

Pharmacy

Eczane

antiseptic	**antiseptik**
Aspirin	**Aspirin**
bandage	**bandaj**
chemist's (UK) pharmacy (US)	**eczane**
condoms	**kondom**
cotton wool	**pamuk**
disinfectant	**dezenfektan**
dose	**doz**
drugstore	**drugstore**
duty chemist	**eczacı**
external use	**harici kullanım**
first - aid box	**ilk yardım çantası**
internal use	**ağızdan kullanım**
medicine	**ilaç**
night service chemist's	**nöbetçi eczane**
plasters	**plaster**
prescription	**reçete**
sanitary pads	**ped**
suppository	**supozituvar**
syrup	**şurup**
tampons	**tampon**
thermometer	**termometre**
vitamins	**vitamin**

A: I don't feel well.
Kendimi iyi hissetmiyorum.

Q: What is your problem?
Probleminiz nedir?

Q: I have a stomachache.
Midem ağrıyor.

Q: Do you have a prescription.
Reçeteniz var mı?

A: Yes I have.
Evet var.

A: Here is a bottle of syrup. Take it two times daily with meals.
Bir şurubunuz var. Günde iki defa yemeklerle birlikte alın.

A: And take these pills three times daily after meals. OK?
Ve bu hapları her gün yemeklerden sonra üç defa bir tane alın.

Q: Are these pills also good for nausea?
Bu ilaçlar bulantıya da iyi gelir mi?

A: I don't think so.
Sanmıyorum.

Post Office

Postane

Turkish post offices are easily recognizable by their yellow **PTT** signs. Major post offices are open from 08:00-24:00 hrs, Mon. - Sat.; and 09:00-06:00 PM. Sun. Small post offices operate during the same hours as government offices, from 09:00-05:00 PM.

It is possible to exchange money at certain **PTT** branches with the current international exchange rate. International postal orders and traveler's checks can also be exchanged.

envelope	**zarf**
express	**ekspres**
gift	**hediye**
letter	**mektup**
ordinary post	**adi posta**
parcel	**paket**
post office	**1. postane** **2. PTT**
post office clerk	**posta memuru**
postal code (UK) zip code (US)	**posta kodu**
postbox	**posta kutusu**
postcards	**1. kart** (shortly) **2. kartpostal**
poste restante	**postrestant**
postman	**postacı**
registered and reply	**iadeli taahhütlü**
reply - paid	**iadeli**
send (v.)	**göndermek**
stamps	**pul**
telegram / cable	**telgraf**

Q: Where is the nearest post office?
En yakın postane nerede?

A: There is one in Taksim, but it is not near here.
Taksim'de var, fakat o buraya çok yakın değil.

A: I want to send this parcel to France.
Bu paketi Fransa'ya göndermek istiyorum.

A: Just a moment please.
Bir dakika lütfen.

Q: Ok, can I help you?
Peki, yardımcı olabilir miyim?

A: I want to send it to Germany.
Bunu Almanya'ya göndermek istiyorum.

Q: How much is it for this parcel by airmail?
Bu paketi uçakla göndermek ne kadar tutar?

A: I have to weigh it up.
Onu tartmak zorundayım.

Q: What is in it?
İçinde ne var?

A: They are some business papers.
Birtakım iş evrakları var.

A: The value is 15 Liras. Fill in this form, please!
On beş Lira tutuyor. Şu formu doldurun lütfen!

A: Thank you.
Teşekkür ederim.

Q: Where can I buy stamps?
Nereden pul alabilirim?

A: Go to the second window.
İkinci gişeye gidin.

* * * * * *

A: Stamps for three postcards to Great Britain, please.
İngiltere'ye üç tane kart için pul lütfen.

Q: By ordinary post or by air mail?
Adi posta mı, yoksa uçakla mı?

A: By air mail.
Uçakla.

Q: How much is an express registered letter?
Ekspres taahhütlü mektup ne kadar?

Q: And three post cards?
Ve üç posta kartı?

A: Your total payment is three and a half Liras.
Toplam ödemeniz üç buçuk Lira.

* * * * * *

A: I want to send a telegraph to USA.
Amerika'ya bir telgraf göndermek istiyorum.

Q: Have you got your text ready?
Göndereceğiniz metin hazır mı?

A: How much is a word?
Kelimesi ne kadar?

A: Fifty Kurus.
Elli Kuruş.

Q: Is it possible to send it express and reply paid?
İadeli ve ekspress göndermek mümkün mü?

A: Yes. You pay two extra Lira for the reply paid.
İadeli için iki Lira fazladan ödeme yaparsınız.

A: Ok. Please register this telegram and give me the receipt.
Tamam. Şu telgrafı kaydedin ve bana bir fiş verin.

* * * * * *

A: Where is the poste restante service in this post office?
Bu postanede postrestant servisi nerede?

A: Go to the third window please.
Lütfen üçüncü gişeye gidin.

A: I should like to ask if there are any letters for me.
Bana bir mektup olup olmadığını öğrenmek istemiştim.

Q: What is your name?
İsminiz nedir?

A: Simon Stern.
Simon Stern.

A: Yes, there are two mails and one postcard for you.
Evet, iki mektup ve bir kartınız var.

Q: And a post card? Thanks.
Kart mı? Teşekkürler.

A: Your identification card please!
Kimliğiniz lütfen!

A: Thank you.
Teşekkür ederim.

Problems

Sorunlar

alone	**1. yalnız** **2. tek başına**
bag	**çanta**
bus	**otobüs**
connection	**1. aktarma** **2. bağlantı**
help (v.)	**yardım etmek**
leave (v.)	**1. ayrılmak** **2. terk etmek**
lose	**kaybetmek**
lost property office	**kayıp eşya bürosu**
matter	**mesele**
miss (v.)	**kaçırmak**
need (v.)	**ihtiyacı olmak**
passport	**pasaport**
platform	**peron**
problem	**1. problem** **2. sorun**
speak (v.)	**konuşmak**
train	**tren**
work (v.)	**çalışmak**

Q: Excuse me! Can you help me?
Afedersiniz! Yardım eder misiniz?

A: Sorry. I only speak a little French.
Özür dilerim. Ben çok az Fransızca konuşurum.

Q: Does anyone here speak English?
Burada İngilizce konuşan biri var mı?

A: What's the matter?
Sorun nedir?

Q: I'm lost. How do I get to The Marmara Hotel?
Kayboldum. The Marmara Oteli'ne nasıl giderim?

A: The Marmara Hotel! It is really far from here.
The Marmara Oteli. Buraya gerçekten çok uzak.

Q: Do I need to take a taxi there?
Bir taksi mi tutmalıyım?

A: Yes. Take a taxi and tell the driver to go to Taksim.
Evet. Bir taksi tutun ve şoföre Taksim'e gitmesini söyleyin.

A: Many thanks.
Çok teşekkürler.

A: You are welcome.
Bir şey değil.

* * * * * *

A: Oh no!!!!
Ooo, Hayır!!!!

Q: What is the matter?
Problem nedir?

A: I missed my train to Pamukkale.
Pamukkale trenini kaçırdım.

Q: Which platform was it?
Hangi perondaydı?

A: It was at the third platform.
Üçüncü perondaydı.

A: Your train is still here!
Sizin treniniz hala burada!

Q: Where is it?
Nerede?

A: At the second platform on the left.
Soldaki ikinci peronda.

A: Really! Sorry. I confused my platform.
Gerçekten mi! Özür dilerim. Ben peronumu karıştırdım.

A: Many thanks for your help.
Yardımlarınız için teşekkürler.

Q: Excuse me! Do you need some help?
Afedersiniz! Yardıma ihtiyacınız var mı?

A: Yes please. I am looking for the lost property office.
Evet. Kayıp eşya bürosunu arıyorum.

Q: Have you lost something?
Bir şey mi kaybettiniz?

A: Yes. I have lost my hand bag.
Evet. Çantamı kaybettim.

Q: Is there any lost property office here?
Burada kayıp eşya bürosu var mı?

A: Unfortunately not.
Ne yazık ki yok.

Q: I need to phone the French consulate. Any public telephone?
Fransız Konsolosluğunu aramalıyım. Hiç umumi telefon var mı?

A: Why don't you come with me? You can call them at my home.
Niye benimle evime gelmiyorsunuz? Onları benim evimden arayabilirsiniz.

A: No thanks. Leave me alone!
Hayır teşekkürler. Beni yalnız bırakın!

Q: What is the problem with you? I am just trying to help you.
Neyiniz var? Ben sadece yardım etmeye çalışıyorum.

A: Go away!
Defolun!

* * * * * *

Q: Can you show me how this machine works?
Bana bu makinenin nasıl çalıştığını gösterebilir misiniz?

A: Did you push the power button.
Açma düğmesine bastınız mı?

Q: I did but, it still doesn't work at all.
Bastım ama, hala çalışmıyor.

A: Check the volume control.
Ses ayarını kontrol edin.

A: Oh no! It doesn't work at all!
Of hayır! Çalışmıyor işte!

Q: Did you try to plug it in?
Fişi takmış mıydınız?

A: Oh! I have forgotten to plug it in. Thank you.
Ah! Fişi takmayı unutmuşum. Teşekkürler.

Reception

Resepsiyon

a double bedroom	**çift yataklı oda**
a single bedroom	**tek yataklı oda**
bathroom	**banyo**
cold water	**soğuk su**
divorced	**boşanmış**
full board	**tam pansiyon**
half board	**yarım pansiyon**
hot water	**sıcak su**
lobby	**lobi**
married	**evli**
reception desk	**resepsiyon masası**
reception office	**resepsiyon bürosu**
receptionist	**resepsiyon görevlisi**
roof	**çatı**
single	**bekar**
widower	**boşanmış erkek**

Q: Can I help you?
Yardım edebilir miyim?

A: I have booked a room for the name Mr. Black.
Mr. Black adına bir oda ayırtmıştım.

A: Oh yes. A single room for two nights.
Ah evet. İki gece için tek kişilik oda.

Q: All right. Do I have to fill up any form?
Peki. Bir form dolduracak mıyım?

A: No, just tell me your first name and last name.
Hayır, sadece isim ve soyadınızı bana söyleyin.

A: My first name and last name are George Black.
Benim adım ve soyadım George Black.

A: I'd like to see the room.
Odamı görmek istiyorum.

A: It's all right. It's bright. Thank you.
Tamam. Çok iyi. Teşekkür ederim.

Q: Is the office still open? I want to leave some money there.
Büro hala açık mı? Biraz para bırakmak istiyorum.

A: Please do come in Mr. Black.
Lütfen içeri girin Bay Black.

Q: Will you keep this money for me, please? Here is my card.
Şu parayı benim için saklayabilir misiniz? İşte kartım.

Q: What is your room number?
Oda numaranız kaç?

A: My room number is 205.
Oda numaram 205 (iki yüz beş).

Q: Are there any messages for me?
Bana mesaj var mı?

A: Yes. A telephone call from your New York office.
Evet. New York ofisinizden aradılar.

A: Ok, I'll call them later. I want to rent a car with a driver.
Tamam, sonra ararım. Şoförlü bir araba kiralamak istiyorum.

Q: Shall I call the rent a car agency now?
Araba kiralama servisini şimdi arayayım mı?

Q: How much do they charge a day?
Günlük ne kadardır?

A: I am not sure. I'll ask them.
Emin değilim. Onlara soracağım.

A: They say it is 25 US Dollars daily.
Günlük 25 Amerikan Doları olduğunu söylüyorlar.

Q: Is everything included?
Her şey dahil mi?

A: Yes.
Evet.

A: That is Ok. Please wake me up early tomorrow morning.
Tamam oldu. Lütfen beni sabah erken uyandırın.

Q: Would you wake me up at half past seven?
Saat yedi buçukta uyandırabilir misiniz?

A: Yes sir, I have noted it down.
Evet. Notunuzu aldım.

A: I'm leaving tomorrow afternoon. Please prepare the bill.
Yarın öğleden sonra ayrılıyorum. Lütfen faturamı hazırlayın.

A: All right Mr. Black. Your bill will be ready.
Peki efendim. Faturanız hazır olacak.

A: The key please.
Anahtar lütfen.

Renting a Car

Araba Kiralama

There are **Rent a Car** companies if you need a car in Turkey. It is possible to make a reservation before you arrive. You can also get help from the agents of airlines and hotels. Before you decide driving a car in Turkey I would like to remind you that Turkish drivers do not obey the traffic rules in general.

driving license	**ehliyet**
car insurance	**kasko**
insurance	**sigorta**
pick-up date	**teslim alma tarihi**
rental date and time	**kiralama tarihi ve zamanı**
return date	**1. geri verme tarihi** **2. iade etme tarihi**

Q: How I can find a car rental agent?
Araba kiralama servisi nasıl bulabilirim?

A: Please ask for the receptionist.
Resepsiyona sorun lütfen.

Q: Could you help me to find a rent a car agent?
Bir araba kiralama servisi bulmama yardım eder misiniz?

A: Here is the agents list.
Servislerin listesi burada.

* * * * * *

Q: Hello, can I help you?
Merhaba, yardım edebilir miyim?

A: I want to hire a car for five days.
Beş günlüğüne bir araba kiralamak istiyorum.

Q: What kind of a car do you wish?
Nasıl bir araba istersiniz?

A: This seems good.
Şu fena görünmüyor.

Q: How much is this car per day? How much is the deposit?
Bu arabanın günlüğü ne kadar? Depozit ne kadar?

A: It is $25 daily and no deposit needed.
Günlük 25 Dolar ve depozit gerekmiyor.

Q: Is there a mileage (kilometer) charge? How much is it?
Kilometre başına herhangi bir ödeme var mı? Ne kadar?

A: No, there is no charge for kilometer.
Hayır, kilometre için ödeme yok.

Q: Does the price include fully comprehensive insurance?
Fiyatın içine tüm sigorta masrafları dahil mi?

A: Yes, our prices include CDW (Collusion Damage Waiver), tax and insuance.
Evet, fiyatlarımıza trafik sigortası, vergiler ve kasko dahildir.

Q: Shall I return the car here? By what time?
Arabayı buraya mı getireceğim? En geç ne zaman?

A: You can return the car at the hotel, we will come and pick it up.
Eğer arabayı otelinize getirirseniz biz sizi orada karşılarız.

A: You can also return the car to our offices.
Arabayı buraya ofise de getirebilirsiniz.

Q: I'd like to leave it in Antalya. Would it be possible?
Ben onu Antalya'da bırakmak istiyorum. Mümkün mü?

A: That is Ok. Just a $75 one way fee is required for one way rentals.
Olabilir. Ancak 75 Dolar geri dönüş bedeli ödemeniz gerekir.

Q: Ok then. Would you please show me how the controls work?
Tamam. Şimdi bana arabanın kullanma özelliklerini anlatın.

A: Ok. Bye for now.
Tamam. Görüşmek üzere.

Restaurant

Lokanta / Restoran

In Turkey, restaurants are called "**lokanta**", but the word "**restoran**" is mostly used instead of "**lokanta**" except for old fashioned places. There aren't many special places for vegetarians, but those preferring vegetarian dishes will not be in trouble in finding something to eat because Turkish meals are rich in vegetables.

FOOD PLACES	
Lokanta	Restaurant
Muhallebici	Old fashioned places. Their menus include deserts prepared by milk. Also some other dishes are available.
Balıkçı Lokantası	Restaurants serving fish and sea food.
Pastane	Cake shops often serving delicious pastries.
Büfe	Take away places. You see every where in big cities.

appetizers	**meze**	lunch	**öğle yemeği**
beef	**dana eti**	meat	**et**
bread	**ekmek**	menu	**menü**
butter	**tereyağı**	no sugar	**1. şekersiz** **2. sade** (coffee,tea)
cheers!	**Şerefe!**	pepper	**biber**
chicken	**tavuk**	plate	**tabak**
cup	**fincan**	salad	**salata**
dessert	**tatlı**	salt	**tuz**
dinner	**akşam yemeği**	soup	**çorba**
fish	**balık**	spoon	**kaşık**
fork	**çatal**	starters	**başlangıçlar**
fruit	**meyva**	sugar	**şeker**
glass	**bardak**	the bill	**hesap**
ice	**buz**	The bill please!	**Hesap lütfen!**
ice cream	**dondurma**	vegetable	**sebze**
knife	**bıçak**	vegetarian	**vejetaryen**

Q: Are there any vegetarian restaurants here?
Burada vejetaryenler için bir lokanta bulunur mu?

A: Unfortunately not. Don't worry about it. You can find a menu rich in vegetables everywhere.
Maalesef yok. Fakat merak etmeyin. Her yerde sebze yemekleri bulabilirsiniz.

Q: Can you recommend a good local restaurant?
İyi bir yerel lokanta tavsiye edebilir misiniz?

A: Yes. I can.
Evet önerebilirim.

Q: I'd like to book a table for three people for tonight.
Bu akşam için üç kişilik bir masa ayırtmak istiyorum.

A: Ok. I'll call the restaurant for you.
Peki. Sizin için restorana telefon edeceğim.

* * * * * *

Q: Have you a set-price menu?
Sabit fiyatlı bir menünüz var mı?

A: Sorry, unfortunately not.
Özür dilerim, maalesef yok.

Q: What is the dish of the day?
Günün yemeği hangisi?

A: Rose beef with some vegetables.
Sebzeli biftek.

Q: Do you have something special to offer?
Önerebileceğiniz özel bir şey var mı?

A: Oh, I suggest you fish.
Ah, size balık öneririm.

Q: Do you have any vegetarian dishes?
Vejetaryen yemekleriniz var mı?

A: Yes. There are some vegetables prepared with olive oil.
Evet. Zeytinyağlı sebzelerimiz var.

Q: Which dishes have no meat or fish?
Hangi yemekler et ve balık içermiyor?

A: You can choose some dishes from the right side of menu.
Menüde sağ taraftaki yemeklerden seçebilirsiniz.

Q: Can you recommend a local dish?
Yerel bir şey önerebilir misiniz?

A: Yaprak Sarmasi is a special dish of Turkish cuisine. I suggest you to taste it.
Yaprak sarması Türk mutfağının özel bir yemeğidir. Denemenizi öneririm.

A: It is made with grape leaves.
Üzüm yaprakları ile hazırlanır.

Q: What is in it?
İçinde ne var?

A: Some rice, raisin and onion. It is also flowered by some spices. It is prepared with olive oil.
Pirinç, kuru üzüm ve soğan. Aynı zamanda baharatla tatlandırılmıştır. Zeytinyağı ile hazırlanmıştır.

Q: Ok, I'll have that.
Peki, ondan istiyorum.

A: OK.
Peki.

Q: Excuse me! May I have some more "yaprak sarmasi"? And more bread please.
Afedersiniz! Biraz daha yaprak sarması rica edebilir miyim? Ve biraz daha ekmek lütfen.

A: Here you are. Anything else?
Buyrun. Başka arzunuz?

A: No thanks. Everything is Ok.
Hayır teşekkürler. Her şey tamam.

Room Service
Oda Servisi

breakfast	**kahvaltı**
clean	**temiz**
coat	**palto**
dinner	**akşam yemeği**
glass	**bardak**
hanger	**askı**
later	**daha sonra**
lunch	**öğle yemeği**
soap	**sabun**
toilet paper	**tuvalet kağıdı**
towel	**havlu**
water	**su**

Q: Room service? What time is the breakfast?
Oda servisi mi? Kahvaltı saat kaçta?

A: From eight to ten o'clock.
Kahvaltı saatleri sekiz ile on arasında.

Q: Can you bring my breakfast to my room?
Kahvaltımı odama getirebilir misiniz?

A: Please come back later.
Lütfen daha sonra gelin.

A: Come in!
Girin!

Q: The breakfast is ready. Anything else?
Kahvaltınız hazır. Başka arzunuz?

A: Please bring clean towels.
Lütfen temiz havlu getirin.

A: Furthermore, I need more cloth hangers.
Ayrıca, biraz daha askıya ihtiyacım var.

A: Ok. I'll bring it right now.
Peki. Hemen getiririm.

Q: Pardon! Do you have a trouser press?
Pardon! Pantolon presi bulunur mu?

A: Yes sir. Please give me your trousers.
Evet beyefendi, lütfen pantolonunuzu verin.

Q: Can I have my shoes cleaned?
Ayakkabılarımı temizletebilir miyim?

A: Yes sir. Please give me your shoes too.
Evet beyefendi. Lütfen ayakkabılarınızı da verin.

Shopping

Alışveriş

What to Buy

Evil eye bead, carpets & kilims, leather made goods, textile goods and jewelry are the best items you can buy in your visit to Turkey. Please check the Suggestions and Warnings section for more information about these items.

bag	**çanta**
button	**düğme**
clothes	**elbise**
cotton	**pamuk**
handbag	**el çantası**
large	**1. büyük** **2. geniş**
leather	**deri**
sale	**ucuzluk**
silk	**ipek**
small	**küçük**
suede	**süet**
suitcase	**bavul**
tight	**dar**
toys	**oyuncak**
wallet / purse	**cüzdan**
wool	**yün**
zip	**fermuar**

Q: Can you recommend me any good shops?
Bana iyi bir alışveriş merkezi önerebilir misiniz?

Q: What kind of shops?
Ne tür bir alışveriş?

A: I'm looking for a present for my girl.
Kızım için bir hediye arıyorum.

Q: Toy shop?
Oyuncakçı mı?

A: I have no idea yet.
Henüz bir fikrim yok.

Q: How do I get to the main shopping area?
Ana alışveriş merkezine nasıl gidebilirim?

A: Ok. Go to the shopping center at the corner of the first traffic lights.
Tamam. İlk trafik ışıklarındaki alışveriş merkezine git.

* * * * * *

Q: Can I help you?
Yardım edebilir miyim?

A: Thank you. I'm just looking.
Teşekkür ederim. Sadece bakıyorum.

Q: Do you have any larger size of this skirt?
Bu eteğin bir beden büyüğü var mı?

A: Yes we have. Here you are bigger one.
Evet var. İşte büyük bedeni.

Q: May I try this on?
Deneyebilir miyim?

A: Sure.
Elbette.

Q: Where are the changing rooms?
Giyinme odaları nerede?

A: Follow me please.
Beni takip edin lütfen.

Q: Excuse me! Do you have this in medium size?
Afedersiniz! Bunun orta bedeni var mı?

Q: What size are you? Does medium size fit you?
Siz kaç bedensiniz? Orta beden size uyar mı?

A: I am 42. But it looks large for me.
42 bedenim. Ama bu bana bol gibi görünüyor.

A: Ok. Let me check the medium size.
Peki. Orta bedeni var mı bir bakayım.

A: Sorry we haven't.
Özür dilerim kalmamış.

Q: Do you have this in some other colors?
Bunun başka renkleri var mı?

A: Sorry, we haven't.
Özür dilerim yok.

Q: Do you have anything else similar to this?
Buna benzer başka bir şeyler var mı?

Q: Yes we have. How about this one.
Evet var. Buna ne dersiniz?

Q: It's too expensive for me. Do you have a little cheaper one?
O çok pahalı. Biraz daha ucuz bir şeyler yok mu?

A: Just a moment please. I'll check a cheaper one for you.
Bir dakika lütfen. Sizin için ucuz bir şeyler bakacağım.

A: Oh, thanks.
Ah, teşekkürler.

Q: It is good, isn't it?
Bu güzel değil mi?

A: Ok. I'll take it.
Tamam. Bunu alıyorum.

Q: Would you like anything else?
Başka bir şeyler ister misiniz?

A: No thanks. That's all.
Hayır teşekkürler. Hepsi bu kadar.

Q: Pardon me! It is me again. Which floor are shoes on?
Pardon. Yine ben! Ayakkabılar hangi katta?

A: Take the second floor.
İkinci kata gidin.

A: Thank you.
Teşekkür ederim.

Shops A-Z

Dükkan ve Mağaza İsimleri A-Z

baker's	**fırın**
bookshop	**kitapçı**
butcher's	**kasap**
department store	**mağaza**
dry-cleaner's	**kuru temizleme**
electrical goods	**elektrikçi**
fishmonger's	**balıkçı**
furniture shop	**mobilyacı**
gift-shop	**hediyelik eşya**
greengrocer	**manav**
grocer's	**bakkal**
hairdresser	**1. kuaför (women)** **2. berber (men)**
jewelery	**kuyumcu**
market	**market**
music-shop	**müzik evi**
pastry-shop	**pastane**
pharmacy (US) chemist's (UK)	**eczane**
shop	**1. dükkan** **2. mağaza**
sports shop	**spor giyim**
stationery	**kırtasiye**
supermarket	**süpermarket**

Sightseeing in Istanbul

İstanbulda Kısa Gezi

Where to Go

You can get information about companies who organize **sightseeing tours** from the local tourist offices. They will have the details of opening hours and the different excursions available in the area. Hotel staff also help you to find a good company.

boat ride	**tekne gezisi**
by boat	**tekneyle**
by bus	**otobüsle**
duration	**süre**
entrance fees	**giriş ücreti**
included	**1. dahil** **2. içinde**
minaret	**minare**
mosque	**cami**
pick up time	**alınış zamanı**
regular tour rate	**standart tur fiyatı**
reservation	**1. rezervasyon** **2. yer ayırtma**
start point	**başlangıç noktası**
tour	**tur**
tour details	**tur detayları**
transfers	**transferler**
travel insurance	**seyahat sigortası**
VAT	**1. K.D.V** **2. Katma değer vergisi**

Q: Where is the tourist office?
Turizm bürosu nerede?

A: It is very close to Blue Mosque.
O Sultanahmet Camisine çok yakın.

A: Excuse me! I'd like to get information about Istanbul tours.
Afedersiniz! İstanbul turları hakkında bilgi almak istiyorum.

Q: What kind of tours are you interested in? By bus or boat.
Hangi turlarla ilgileniyorsunuz. Otobüsle mi, tekneyle mi?

Q: What kind of options do I have?
Hangi seçeneklerimiz var?

A: There are several options and many companies.
Çeşitli seçenekler ve birçok firma var.

Q: Do you have any leaflets about them?
Onlarla ilgili broşürleriniz var mı?

A: Sure. There should be some. Here you are.
Elbette. Şurada bazıları olacak. İşte buyrun.

A: Thanks, bye.
Teşekkürler. Hoşça kalın.

* * * * * *

A: Hello! We are interested in your daily tours.
Merhaba! Biz günlük turlarınızla ilgileniyoruz.

A: We'd like to get in the tour including Spice Bazaar.
Mısır Çarşısını içeren turunuza katılmak istiyoruz.

Q: Spice Bazaar, Rumeli Fortress and Dolmabahce Palace?
Mısır Çarşısı, Rumeli Hisarı ve Dolmabahçe Sarayı?

A: Yes. It is by coach isn't it?
Evet. O tur otobüsle değil mi?

Q: That is right. Which day fits you?
Evet. Size hangi gün uyar?

A: Spice Bazaar is closed on Sundays; Rumeli Fortress is closed on Wednesdays; Dolmabahce Palace is closed on Mondays and Thursdays.
Mısır Çarşısı Pazar günleri, Rumeli Hisarı Çarşamba günleri, Dolmabahçe Sarayı Pazartesi ve Perşembe günleri kapalı.

Q: Tuesdays is good for us. How about the prices?
Salı günü bizim için uygun. Fiyatlar ne civarda?

A: $15 each.
Kişi başı on beş Amerikan Doları.

Q: Any discount for children?
Çocuklar için hiç indiriminiz var mı?

A: Yes. It is $12 for children and students.
Evet. Çocuklar ve öğrenciler on ikişer Amerikan Doları.

Q: Is the VAT (Value Added Tax) included? Any other additional payments?
KDV dahil mi? Herhangi bir ek ödeme var mı?

A: Sure. 17 % VAT (Value Added Tax) included in our prices.
Evet % 17 (yüzde on yedi) KDV fiyatlarımıza dahildir.

Q: Is there any extra charge?
Başka ek bir ödeme var mı?

A: There is no extra charge. Transfers, entrance fees, lunch are included.
Hiçbir ek ödeme yok. Transferler, giriş ücretleri, öğle yemeği dahildir.

A: The travel insurance is also included in our prices.
Seyahat sigortası da fiyatlarımıza dahildir.

Q: Are there any excursions?
Kısa gezintiler de var mı?

A: Sure. Sport shoes are recommended.
Elbette. Spor ayakkabılarla gelmeniz tavsiye edilir.

Q: When do you pick us up from the hotel?
Saat kaçta otelden alıyorsunuz?

A: We pick you up from your hotel at 08:00 am.
Sabah sekizde otelinizden alırız.

Q: Where does it leave from?
Otobüs nereden kalkar?

A: It leaves from Sultanahmet.
Sultanahmet Meydanı'ndan kalkar.

Q: When does it leave?
Ne zaman kalkar?

A: At 09:00 am. from Sultanahmet Square.
Saat dokuzda Sultanahmet Meydanı'ndan.

Q: When can we visit Spice Bazaar?
Mısır Çarşısı'nı ne zaman ziyaret edeceğiz?

A: In the morning before lunch.
Öğle yemeğinden önce, sabahleyin.

Q: When is the return time?
Dönüş saati ne zaman?

A: In the evening around 19:00 pm. we will return to Sultanahmet and you will be transferred to the hotel.
Akşam on dokuz da Sultanahmet'e döneceğiz ve otelinize transfer edileceksiniz.

Q: How much does it cost for three adults and two children?
Üç yetişkin ve iki çocuk için ne kadar tutar?

A: It costs you just $69.
Size sadece 69 (altmış dokuz) Amerikan Doları'na mal olur.

Q: That is Ok. We'd like to get in. Is any deposit needed?
Tamam. Biz katılmak istiyoruz. Depozit gerekli mi?

A: Yes sir. 50% of total cost.
Evet beyefendi. Toplam fiyatın % 50 (yüzde ellisi).

Q: Ok. Here you are.
Tamam. Buyrun.

A: Thank you. We'll pick you up from your hotel, on Tuesday at 08:00 am.
Teşekkür ederim. Sizi Salı günü sabah sekizde otelinizden alacağız.

A: Thanks. See you!
Teşekkürler, görüşmek üzere!

Signs & Notices

İşaret ve Uyarılar

basement	**bodrum**
broken	**bozuk**
cash desk	**ödeme**
closed	**kapalı**
cold	**soğuk**
drinking water	**içecek su**
emergency	**acil**
emergency exit	**acil çıkış**
engaged	**1. meşgul** **2. dolu**
entrance	**giriş**
entrance ticket	**giriş bileti**
exit	**çıkış**
for sale	**satılık**
gate	**kapı**
gents	**bay**
ground floor	**giriş katı**
hospital	**hastane**
hot	**sıcak**
information	**danışma**
lady	**bayan**
left luggage	**emanet**
lift / elevator	**asansör**
no bathing	**yüzülmez**
no entry	**girilmez**
No smoking!	**Sigara içmeyiniz!**
no vacancies	**boş yer yok**
open	**açık**
pull	**çekiniz**
push	**itiniz**
ring	**zil**
roof	**çatı**

sale	**ucuzluk**
self - service	**self - servis**
ticket office	**bilet gişesi**
to rent	**kiralamak**
vacant	**boş**

Stationery A-Z

Kırtasiye Sözlüğü

biro	**tükenmez kalem**
card	**kart**
crayon	**renkli kalem**
envelope	**zarf**
folder	**dosya**
glue	**1. tutkal** **2. zamk**
ink	**mürekkep**
ink cartridge	**mürekkep kartuşu**
magazine	**dergi**
newspaper	**gazete**
note pad	**not ped**
paper	**kağıt**
paperclip	**1. ataş** **2. klips**
pen	**1. dolma kalem** **2. tükenmez kalem**
pencil	**kurşun kalem**
pencil sharpener	**1. kalem açacağı** **2. kalemtıraş**
postcard	**kartpostal**
rubber	**silgi**
ruler	**cetvel**
staple	**zımba teli**
stapler	**tel zımba**

Taxi

Taksi

Taxis can be found in the streets in big cities and are recognizable by their bright yellow color in Turkey. It is also possible to call from the taxi stations. The fare shown on the taximeter reads according to the distance traveled. From midnight (24:00) to morning (06:00) it will cost 50% more than the daytime fare. In general most taxis do not give receipts. If you need a receipt, please ask the driver if he can give you one before you get on the taxi.

attend (v.)	**katılmak**
call (v.)	**çağırmak**
catch up (v.)	**yetişmek**
centre	**merkez**
get on (v.)	**binmek**
hurry	**acele**
leave (v.)	**terk etmek**
take (v.)	**tutmak** (taksi)
taxi	**taksi**
taxi driver	**taksi şoförü**
taximeter	**taksimetre**

A: I would like to call for a taxi.
Bir taksi çağırmak istiyorum.

A: Please tell the receptionist.
Lütfen resepsiyona söyleyin.

Q: Would you please call me a taxi?
Bana bir taksi çağırır mısınız?

A: Sorry, there is no taxi there at the moment.
Özür dilerim, şu anda hiç taksi kalmamış.

Q: Where can I get a taxi?
Nereden bir taksi bulabilirim?

A: You can call one on the street.
Caddeden bir tane çevirebilirsiniz.

A: Taxi!
Taksi!

A: Please take me to this address.
Lütfen beni şu adrese götürün.

A: I am afraid there is a traffic jam on this direction.
Korkarım o istikamette yoğun bir trafik var.

Q: Is the address far from here?
O adres buraya uzak mı?

A: Yes, it is at least 30 kilometers from here.
Evet, en az 30 (otuz) kilometre.

A: I'm in a hurry. Please be quick.
Acelem var. Biraz çabuk lütfen.

Q: What can I do? This is the traffic jam.
Ne yapabilirim? Trafik sıkışık.

A: I have a meeting starting at 03:00 pm.
Saat üçte başlayan bir toplantım var.

Q: Would you like to try the metro?
Metroyu denemek ister misiniz?

Q: How can I find the address from there?
Oradan adresi nasıl bulacağım?

A: Get off from the metro at Levent and take another taxi.
Levent'te metrodan inin ve başka bir taksi tutun.

A: Ok then. Leave me to the nearest metro station.
Peki öyleyse. Beni en yakın metro istasyonunda bırakın.

Q: Do you have smaller banknotes?
Bozuk paranız yok mu?

A: I'm afraid, I've nothing smaller.
Korkarım daha küçük param yok.

A: Ok. Here is the metro station.
Peki. İşte metro istasyonu.

A: Many thanks.
Teşekkürler.

Telephone Call

Telefon Etmek

The country code of Turkey is **+90**. The area code of European side of Istanbul is 0 212 and Anatolian side of Istanbul is 0 216. Ankara's city code is 0 312 and Izmir's city code is 0 232. You should then dial the telephone number. Please check the other International Codes from:

http://www.internationalcodes.com/

The most economic way to telephone in Turkey is from a PTT telephone booth. Phone tokens "**Jeton**" are in three sizes for local, inter-city and international calls and can be purchased from all PTT offices. **Telephone cards** are also available and more practical. To make a long distance call from Turkey, the prefix is **0** for intercity and it is **00** for International calls.

area code	**alan kodu**
card - operated payphone	**kartlı telefon**
coin - operated payphone	**jetonlu telefon**
reverse charge call	**ödemeli arama**
earphone	**kulaklık**
extension	**dahili**
operator	**santral**
phone card	**telefon kartı**
receiver	**ahize**
telephone book	**telefon rehberi**
telephone booth	**telefon kabini**
telephone box	**telefon kulübesi**
telephone directory	**telefon rehberi**
token	**jeton**

A: A token, please.
Bir jeton lütfen.

Q: I want to make a long distance call. May I use this telephone?
Şehirlerarası bir görüşme yapmak istiyorum. Bu telefonu kullanabilir miyim?

A: Sorry. It doesn't work with token. You need a phone card.
Üzgünüm. O jetonla çalışmaz. Telefon kartı alın.

Q: Where can I buy a phone card?
Telefon kartı nereden alabilirim?

A: Ask for the buffet / kiosk up there.
Şuradaki büfeye sorun.

Q: Could you tell me the telephone number for inquiries?
Bilinmeyen numaraların telefonunu söyler misiniz?

A: Please call to 118.
Lütfen 118' i arayın.

Q: How does this telephone work?
Bu telefon nasıl çalışır?

A: Please insert your card.
Lütfen kartınızı sokun.

Q: 0-352-212-00-55? Zero - three hundred fifty two - two hundred and twelve - double zero - fifty five?
Sıfır - üç yüz elli iki - iki yüz on iki - çift sıfır - elli beş mi?

A: Sorry, wrong number.
Özür dilerim, yanlış numara.

Q: What number should I dial?
Hangi numarayı çevirmeliyim.

A: 0352-212-00-56. Please dial the last number as six.
0352-212-00-56. Lütfen son rakamı altı olarak çevirin.

A: The line is busy.
Hatlar meşgul.

Q: Who is speaking, who are you calling?
Kimsiniz, kimi aradınız?

Q: May I speak to Mr. Kaya please?
Kaya Beyle görüşebilir miyim?

Q: Could you say that more slowly?
Lütfen biraz yavaş konuşur musunuz?

Q: Is Mr. Kaya there?
Kaya Bey orada mı?

Q: Do you know his extension number?
Dahili numarasını biliyor musunuz?

A: Please, put me through to extension 112.
Lütfen beni 112'ye bağlayın.

Q: Sorry, who is calling?
Özür dilerim, kim arıyordu?

A: This is Michelle Vise. I am calling from Istanbul.
Michelle Vise. İstanbul'dan arıyorum.

Q: Will it take long?
Bağlanmam uzun sürecek mi?

A: Hold on. Don't hang up, please.
Hatta kalın. Lütfen kapatmayın.

Q: I have difficulty in hearing you. Could you say it louder?
Sizi duyamıyorum. Daha yüksek sesle konuşur musunuz?

A: There is no answer.
Telefonu cevap vermiyor.

Q: Will he come back soon?
Dönüşü gecikir mi?

A: I don't know when he gets back. Please call back later.
Ne zaman döner bilmiyorum. Lütfen daha sonra tekrar arayın.

Q: Could I leave a message?
Mesaj bırakabilir miyim?

A: Sure.
Elbette.

Q: Our meeting is delayed.
Toplantımız ertelendi.

A: Ok. I'll tell him your message.
Peki. Mesajınızı ona söylerim.

A: Many thanks. I'll call him back again.
Teşekkürler. Ben onu tekrar ararım.

Television

Televizyon

TRT which is the only official authority of public service has 7 television channels. These are: TRT1 (general public and diverse broadcasting); TRT2 (culture and art); and TRT3 (the youth channel identity with different types of music programs and sports programs). TRT3 (broadcasts from Parliament). TRT4 (an educational channel which includes the Open University) TRT-INT and TRT-AVRASYA (broadcasts abroad). Furthermore, the GAP-TV (broadcasts in the Southeastern Anatolia Region).

A total of 244 private TV networks, of which 15 are regional and 229 local have applied to the Supreme Council of Radio and Television **(RTÜK)** for licenses in the country.

A total of 1180 radio stations are active in the country. Private radio stations and television channels finance themselves. Their only income sources are advertisements.

ads	**reklamlar**
cartoons	**çizgi film**
children programs	**çocuk programları**
comedy	**komedi**
drama	**drama**
documentary films	**belgesel filmler**
educational programs	**eğitim programları**
entertainment	**eğlence**
horror films	**korku filmleri**
movies	**filmler**
news	**haberler**
remote control	**uzaktan kumanda**
satellite	**uydu**
series	**dizi**
sporting programs	**spor programları**
switch off (v.)	**kapatmak**
switch on (v.)	**açmak**
theme	**konu**
video recorder	**video**

Q: What's on television?
Televizyonda neler var?

A: Would you please switch it on.
Lütfen televizyonu açar mısın?

Q: How do I switch it on?
Nasıl açacağım?

A: Please, use the remote control.
Lütfen uzaktan kumandayı kullan.

Q: Which button do I press?
Hangi düğmeye basacağım?

A: Push the green button on the top.
Üstteki yeşil düğmeye bas.

Q: May I turn the volume up?
Sesini açabilir miyim?

Q: Do you have any English-speaking programs?
İngilizce programlar var mı?

A: Jump to the twenty fifth channel.
Yirmi beşinci kanala geç.

Q: When is the news?
Haberler nasıl?

A: There is hourly short news.
Saat başı kısa haberler var.

Q: Do you have any Turkish videos?
Türkçe video filmin var mı?

A: Just the children programs I have.
Sadece çocuklar için var bende.

Q: They may help me to improve my Turkish.
Türkçemi geliştirmeme yardımcı olabilirler.

Tender Words

Şefkat Sözcükleri

My sun.

Güneşim.

My love.

Aşkım.

My dear.

Sevgilim.

My angel.

Meleğim.

My little girl.

Küçüğüm.

My sweet.

Tatlım.

My sweetheart.

Canım.

You are so beautiful.

Çok güzelsin.

You are so wonderful.

Harikasın.

You are so splendid.

Muhteşemsin.

You are so exciting.

Çok heyecan vericisin.

You are so lovely.

Çok güzelsin.

You are so pretty.

Çok sevimlisin.

You are so cute.

Çok şekersin.

You are so sweet.

Çok tatlısın.

You are so sensitive.

Çok duyarlısın.

You are so sentimental.

Çok duygusalsın.

You are so talented.

Çok yeteneklisin.

You are so wise.

Çok akıllısın.

You are so understanding.

Çok anlayışlısın.

You are so soft.

Çok yumuşaksın.

You are so gentle.

Çok naziksin.

You are so delightful.

1. Çok zevklisin.

2. Hoşsun.

You are so devoted.

Çok sadıksın.

You are so unusual.

Sen sıra dışı birisin.

You are so honest.

Çok dürüstsün.

You are so sincere.

Çok candansın.

You are so kind.

1. Çok kibarsın.

2. İyi kalplisin.

You are so open.

1. Çok içtensin.

2. Dürüstsün.

You are so glamorous.

Çok çekicisin.

You are so engaging.
Çok alımlısın.

You are so heavenly.
Nefissin.

You are so gifted.
Çok yeteneklisin.

Time Expressions

Zaman İfadeleri

as soon as possible	**en kısa zamanda**
at about 10 o'clock	**yaklaşık saat onda**
century	**1. yüzyıl** **2. asır**
decade	**onyıl**
early	**erken**
in a while	**bir süre içinde**
in an hour's time	**bir saat içinde**
in the afternoon	**öğleden sonra**
in the evening	**akşam**
in the morning	**sabahleyin**
last year	**1. geçen yıl** **2. geçen sene**
late	**geç**
later	**daha sonra**
next year	**1. gelecek yıl** **2. gelecek sene**
nine o'clock at the latest	**en geç saat dokuzda**
soon	**yakında**
the day after tomorrow	**yarından sonra**
the day before yesterday	**1. önceki gün** **2. evvelki gün**
this afternoon	**bu öğleden sonra**
this morning	**bu sabah**
this year	**1. bu yıl** **2. bu sene**
today	**bugün**
tomorrow	**yarın**
tomorrow evening	**yarın akşam**
tomorrow morning	**yarın sabah**
tomorrow night	**yarın gece**
tonight	**bu akşam**
yesterday	**dün**

Train

Tren

In general trains are cheaper than buses. Please remember that bus travel is usually faster than the train.

Foremost Trains and Routes
Ankara Ekspresi: İstanbul (Haydarpaşa) - Ankara
Boğaziçi Ekspresi: İstanbul (Haydarpaşa) - Ankara
Pamukkale Ekspresi: İstanbul (Haydarpaşa) - Denizli (Pamukkale)
Meram Ekspresi: İstanbul (Haydarpasa) - Konya
For more information please visit **http://www.tcdd.gov.tr/**

car	**vagon**
compartment	**kompartıman**
couchettes	**kuşet**
double	**çift**
large rail way station	**gar**
passenger cars	**yolcu kompartımanı**
platform	**peron**
pullman	**pulman**
rail way station	**tren istasyonu**
return ticket	**gidiş - dönüş bilet**
route	**1. yön** **2. rota** **3. istikamet**
single	**tek**
sleeping cars	**yataklı vagon**
ticket	**bilet**
train	**tren**

Q: Is there a train to Izmir?
İzmir'e tren bulunur mu?

A: Sorry, I am not sure. Please ask for the information.
Özür dilerim, emin değilim. Danışmaya sorun.

Q: When is the first train to Izmir?
İzmir'e ilk tren ne zaman?

A: There is no train directly going to Izmir.
İzmir'e direkt giden bir tren yok.

Q: Do I need to change? Where?
Aktarma mı yapacağım? Nerede?

A: There is a boat from Istanbul to Bandirma in connection with the train to Izmir.
İzmir trenine aktarmalı İstanbul'dan Bandırma'ya giden bir gemi var.

Q: When does it arrive to Bandirma?
Bandırma'ya ne zaman varır?

A: At 11:00 pm.
Gece saat on birde.

Q: Is there a sleeping car option?
Yataklı vagon seçeneği var mı?

A: Unfortunately not.
Ne yazık ki yok.

A: Ok. A single ticket to Izmir, please.
Peki. İzmir'e tek kişilik bilet lütfen.

Q: Does the train to Denizli depart from here?
Denizli treni buradan mı kalkar?

A: Yes.
Evet.

Q: Does the train stop in Eskisehir?
Eskişehir'de durur mu?

A: Yes, but be careful! It just hangs about five minutes.
Evet, fakat dikkatli olun. Orada sadece beş dakika oyalanır.

Q: When is the next train to Denizli?
Denizli'ye bir sonraki tren ne zaman?

A: You have just one option to Denizli. It is Pamukkale Express.
Sadece tek seçeneğiniz var. O da Pamukkale Ekspresi.

Q: Ok. I want to buy tickets for the Pamukkale Express.
Peki. Pamukkale Ekspresi için bilet alacağım.

Q: For how many people?
Kaç kişilik?

A: Two return tickets please.
İki tane gidiş-dönüş bilet lütfen.

A: Here you are.
Buyrun.

Q: Which platform does it leave from?
Hangi perondan kalkar?

A: Please go to the third platform.
Üçüncü platforma gidin lütfen.

Q: When will it leave?
Kaçta hareket eder?

A: At 06:00 pm.
Saat altıda.

Q: When does it arrive to Denizli?
Denizli'ye ne zaman varır?

A: At 08:00 am, tomorrow morning.
Yarın, sabah sekizde.

A: That is Ok. Thanks.
Tamam. Teşekkürler.

Q: Excuse me, is this the train for Denizli?
Afedersiniz, bu Denizli treni mi?

A: Yes.
Evet.

Q: Is this free? (seat)
Burası boş mu?

A: Sorry it is taken. You can take next one.
Özür dilerim, boş değil. Yanındakine oturabilirsiniz.

Q: Is there a buffet on the train?
Trende hiç büfe var mı?

A: There is a restaurant on the second car.
İkinci vagonda lokanta var.

A: Please let me know when we get to Eskisehir.
Lütfen Eskişehir'e gelince haber verin.

A: OK.
Peki.

Vegetables

Sebzeler

The plant cover is really rich in Turkey. Most vegetables are natural and fresh. I suggest you to prefer seasonal vegetable dishes prepared by olive oil. You can find them in all restaurants. These vegetable dishes are usually eaten cold and really healthy.

artichoke	**enginar**
asparagus	**kuşkonmaz**
aubergine (UK) eggplant (US)	**patlıcan**
bean	**fasulye**
broad bean	**bakla**
cabbage	**lahana**
carrot	**havuç**
cauliflower	**karnabahar**
celery	**kereviz**
cucumber	**salatalık**
dill	**dereotu**
garden cress	**tere**
garlic	**sarımsak**
green pepper	**biber**
Jerusalem artichoke	**yerelması**
kidney - bean	**börülce**
leek	**pırasa**
lettuce	**marul**
mint	**nane**
okra	**bamya**
onion	**soğan**
parsley	**maydanoz**
pea	**bezelye**
purslane	**semizotu**
radish	**turp**
red pepper	**kırmızı biber**
reddish colored bean	**barbunya fasulye**
spinach	**ıspanak**
tomato	**domates**

Weather

Hava Durumu

Temperature Units Conversion:
Celsius to Fahrenheit Conversion
[Celsius degrees] x 9 : 5 + 32
Fahrenheit to Celsius Conversion:
[Fahrenheit degrees] - 32 x 5 : 9

Please visit **Fahrenheit to Celsius Converter** page which helps you to convert temperatures online: **http://www.wbuf.noaa.gov/tempfc.htm**

awful	**berbat**
cold	**soğuk**
hot	**sıcak**
lovely	**1. harika** **2. güzel**
rain (n.)	**yağmur**
rain (v.)	**yağmur yağmak**
rainy (adj.)	**1. yağmurlu** **2. yağışlı**
snow (n.)	**kar**
snow (v.)	**kar yağmak**
snowy (adj.)	**1. kar yağışlı** **2. karlı**
stop (v.)	**durmak**
storm	**fırtına**
sun (n.)	**güneş**
sunny (adj.)	**güneşli**
temperature	**1. hava sıcaklığı** **2. sıcaklık**
umbrella	**şemsiye**
warm	**ılık**
weather	**hava**
weather forecast	**hava tahmini**
wind (v.)	**rüzgar esmek**
windy	**rüzgarlı**

A: What a lovely day!
Ne güzel bir gün!

Q: What will the weather be like tomorrow?
Hava yarın nasıl olacak?

A: It's sunny again, but a little windy.
Yine güneşli, fakat biraz rüzgarlı.

Q: What is the temperature?
Kaç derece?

A: The weather is very hot. Nearly 31°C (degree Celsius).
Hava çok sıcak. Neredeyse 31 derece.

Q: Do you think it will snow in Erzurum?
Erzurum'da kar yağacağını düşünüyor musun?

A: I don't think so. It is early to snow.
Sanmıyorum. Kar için erken.

Q: Do you think there will be a storm?
Fırtına olacağını düşünüyor musun?

A: I don't think so.
Sanmıyorum.

A: But it is snowing in Ağrı.
Ama Ağrı'da kar yağıyor.

Q: When will it stop snowing up there?
Orada kar yağışı ne zaman durur?

A: It will stop soon.
Yakında durur.

Q: Will it start to rain?
Yağmur mu başlayacak?

A: Yes, it seems to rain soon.
Evet, birazdan yağmur başlayacak gibi.

Q: Do I need an umbrella?
Şemsiyeye ihtiyacım olur mu?

A: I suggest you to get your umbrella with you.
Sana şemsiyeni yanına almanı öneririm.

A: What an awful weather! It changes hourly.
Ne berbat hava! Saat başı değişiyor.

Q: Is it raining ?
Yağmur mu yağıyor?

A: Yes, it is.
Evet, yağıyor.

What time is it?

Saat kaç?

09:30	**Saat dokuz buçuk.**	It is half past nine.
09:30	**Saat dokuz otuz.**	It is nine thirty.
09:45	**Saat ona çeyrek var.**	It is a quarter to ten.
09:45	**Saat dokuz kırk beş.**	It is nine forty five.
08:20	**Saat sekizi yirmi geçiyor.**	It is twenty past eight.
08:20	**Saat sekiz buçuğa on var.**	It is ten to eight thirty.
12:30	**Saat yarım.**	It is half past twelve.
12:30	**Saat on iki otuz.**	It is half past twelve.
03:36	**Saat üçü otuz altı geçiyor.**	It is thirty six past three.
08:05	**Saat sekizi beş geçiyor**	It is five past eight.
08:05	**Saat Sekizi beş dakika geçiyor**	It is five minutes past eight.

Q: Sabahları kaçta kalkarsın?
At what time do you get up in the mornings?

A: Sabahları yedi otuzda kalkarım.
I get up at seven thirty in the mornings.

A: Sabahları yedi buçukta kalkarım.
I get up at half past seven in the mornings.

Q: Saat kaçta kahvaltı edersiniz?
At what time do you have breakfast?

A: Ben genellikle saat sekize çeyrek kala kahvaltı ederim.
I usually have breakfast at quarter to eight.

A: Ben genellikle yediyi kırkbeş geçe kahvaltı ederim.
I usually have breakfast at forty five past seven.

A: Ben genellikle yedi kırk beşte kahvaltı ederim.
I usually have breakfast at seven-forty five.

Q: Geceleri kaçta yatarsın?
At what time do you go to bed?

A: Ben bazen saat on biri yirmi geçe yatarım.
I sometimes go to bed at twenty past eleven.

A: Ben bazen on bir buçuğa on kala yatarım.
I sometimes go to bed at ten to eleven thirty.

A: Ben bazen on bir yirmide yatarım.
I sometimes go to bed at eleven twenty.

Q: O akşam yemeğini kaçta yer.
At what time does he eat dinner?

A: O akşam yemeklerini yediyi çeyrek geçe yer.
He eats dinner at quarter past seven.

A: O ender olarak akşam yemeğini yedi buçukta yer.
He rarely eats dinner at half past seven.

SUGGESTIONS AND WARNINGS

ÖNERİLER VE UYARILAR

Communication

İletişim

The country code of Turkey is **+90**. The area code of European side of Istanbul is **0 212** and Anatolian side of Istanbul is **0 216**. Ankara's city code is **0 312** and Izmir's city code is **0 232**. You should then dial the telephone number. Please check the other **International Codes** by visiting **http://www.internationalcodes.com/**

The most economic way to telephone in Turkey is from a PTT telephone booth. Phone tokens **(Jeton)** are in three sizes for local, inter-city and international calls and can be purchased from all PTT offices. **Telephone cards** are also available and more practical. To make a long distance call from Turkey, the prefix is **0** for intercity and it is **00** for International calls.

Turkish post offices are easily recognizable by their yellow PTT signs. Major post offices are open from 08:00 - 24:00 hrs, Mon. - Sat.; and 09:00 AM - 05:00 PM, Sun. Small post offices operate during the same hours as government offices, from 09:00 AM - 05:00 PM

It is possible to exchange money at certain **PTT** branches with the current international exchange rate. International postal orders and traveler's checks can also be exchanged.

E-MAIL: Turkey is a paradise of Internet Cafes where you can use the computers to access the Internet while you pay a fee charged per hour.

WARNINGS:

- **At hotels telephone prices and connecting to internet are high, so take it under your consideration.**
- **If you intend to use your calling card at your hotel, check whether they charge an extra price for it.**

Cigarette smoking

Sigara İçme

Although, smoking is forbidden by law in official and some public places it is a popular national and social activity throughout Turkey. So, the law is not put into practice in general. There are restaurants which have separate non-smoking areas.

WARNINGS:

- **Ask for waiters an appropriate place for smoking.**
- **If you want to tell a particular person not to smoke tell it in a very polite way, smokers don't like hearing such words.**

Driving

Araba Kullanma

Parking is a serious problem in big cities of Turkey. I suggest all visitors to get information about parking before you intend to go any place by your car. Maybe taking a taxi will be more useful in the cities.

Driving a rental car gives you the freedom to enjoy the countryside and coastline. There are Rent a Car companies if you need a car in Turkey. It is possible to make a reservation before you arrive. You can also get help from the agents of airlines and hotels.

WARNINGS:

- **Before you decide using a car in Turkey I would like to remind you that Turkish drivers do not obey the traffic rules in general.**
- **Avoid driving at night and get your gas before you enter a toll-highway if possible. And, be sure that you have a good road map with you.**

Electricity

Elektrik

Plugs are of the European variety with two round prongs. Take your adapter with you if you intend to take any electrical appliances with you. Electricity in Turkey:

- Is supplied at 220 volts, 50 cycles, as in Europe.
- Plugs are European round / 2-prong plug.

Food Water & Other Drinks

Yiyecek Su ve Diğer İçecekler

It is sad that tap water is no longer safe to drink in all cities, although it has been chlorinated. I suggest you bottled water because of the compounds in tap water may be different in each country. There is no restriction in selling or drinking of alcohol.

WARNINGS:

- **Drink only mineral water or bottled water.**
- **Do not doubt about water supplied on food, because the water is boiled.**
- **Be careful in taking alcohol during the month RAMADAN in small places, because a lot of Turkish people do fast.**

Health

Sağlık

Before you come to Turkey no immunization is required. The most common medical problem that a visitor may experience is the 'Travelers Diarrhea'.

WARNINGS:

- **Please consult your physician beforehand and get prepared by taking appropriate pills with you for Diarrhea.**

Money & Valuables

Para ve Değerli Şeyler

Turkish Lira

Türk Lirası

The Turkish Lira has been converted starting 01 January 2005. The national monetary unit was the Turkish Lira (TL). The amounts were in 50,000, 100,000 and 250,000 Lira denominations. Bank notes were of 500,000, 1,000,000, 5,000,000, 10,000,000, and 20,000,000 Liras.

The new currency unit of the Republic of Turkey is the New Turkish Lira. One million Turkish Lira (1.000.000 TL) is equivalent to one New Turkish Lira (1 NTL). In other words, 6 zeros has been dropped from our currency. The sub-unit of New Turkish Lira is "New Kuruş". One New Turkish Lira (NTL) is equivalent to a hundred New Kuruş (NKr). Current banknotes and coins will be in circulation until the end of 2005.

Exchange offices in tourist areas are generally open until midnight and the exchange rates for foreign currencies are published daily. All major credit cards are accepted.

Exchange Services and Rates:

Para Değiştirme ve Kurlar

You can exchange major currencies in two ways. You can use banks or exchange offices **(DÖVİZ)**, both of which can be found in the city center. Generally choosing these exchange companies will be profitable than the banks. Exchange offices are open for longer hours than banks and do not charge commission. Many are open also on Saturdays.

Cash Dispensers:

ATM'ler

Cash dispensers (ATM - Automatic Teller Machines) usually do not let you choose which language to carry out the transaction in. Also, in smaller places, you might have trouble finding the one that takes your card. You can exchange money in the branches of banks (Monday-Friday, open from 08:30 AM to noon & from 01:30 PM to 05:00 PM) which are entitled to exchange money. However, they charge a commission. In the receptions of the hotels you can do it as well but they charge you even a higher commission. There are also privately owned small exchange offices on the main streets of the big cities. They are open on weekdays and usually do not charge a commission. The Turkish word for exchange is **"Döviz"**. Exchange rate changes from one bank to another, from one office to another.

Travelers' checks are seen as a burden to change so only more expensive hotels and shops accept them but not at good rates of exchange. There is no currency black market in Turkey. So keep away any susceptible person who says so. Big hotels, the more expensive shops and car rental agencies accept your credit card but make sure in advance because not all establishments accept all cards. Shopkeepers may require you to pay the credit card fee from 3% to 7%, or the charges for making credit card arrangements with the bank. There are ATMs which pay out money from your account when you insert your credit or cash card and secret password. But these are the big city advantages and you must be certain they will work. You would better show your card to the bank's officers first.

WARNINGS:

- **When traveling do not bring your valuables because at any time, or anywhere, you could be robbed (just as in your home country).**
- **I recommend you to use the hotel safety deposit boxes in any part of the world.**

Photograph taking

Fotoğraf Çekme

Do not photograph anything military, whether or not you see signs reading **"Fotoğraf çekmek yasaktır"** or **"Fotoğraf çekilmez"**. If you want to take close-ups of people, ask for their permission beforehand. In the museums please look for the signs posted for photography. In certain places like the rock carved churches of Cappadocia Region photography is strictly forbidden.

Theft And Robbery

Hırsızlık ve Soygun

"I am honored to be a member of my country where no crimes are recorded for more than 50 years in thousands of small towns and villages with no keys on front doors..."

That was what I had written on the top of the related links pages of Turkey in my website. These words are still true for most small towns and villages in Turkey. As a person who was born in a small town in the south part of Turkey, I am still missing such natural security conditions and the happiness of being in a secure atmosphere. I wish we could have been able to save our culture and good features of us. Although, theft is still not much of a problem and robbery is even less compared to most countries, please take these precautions.

WARNINGS:

- **Pay extra attention in the crowded places of Istanbul.**
- **It is recommended for women to leave their handbags in their hotels and put their wallets in a safe place of which they can keep track.**
- **It is also recommended women do not wander around empty and dark streets at night.**
- **Men traveling alone also should be careful at night clubs where they can be in a trap with fun girls.**

Time Zone

Zaman Dilimi

Turkish time is East European Time, two hours ahead of Coordinated Universal Time.

Local time:

GMT: 2 hrs. (Summer)

GMT: 3 hrs. (Winter)

Tipping

Bahşiş

Tipping - addition of a service charge of 10 to 15% to your bill- expected:

- In restaurants
- In hotels

If the service charge is added to your bill, an extra 5 % would be better to be left directly to the waiter.

After your tour, tipping is not expected unless the drivers spend an extra effort for carrying your luggage and suitcases. You do not have to pay a separate fee for the luggage, but a tip is expected if you use the luggage section at the back of the taxi.

Toilets

Tuvaletler

The public toilets are usually not free. You have to pay a small fee to the person who is taking care of the toilet. There are two kinds of toilets one being the ala-turca style and the other is the one you are familiar with. Actually if you do not have problems with your knees, the previous one in a public toilet is more recommendable for hygienic reasons.

WARNINGS:

- **Please ask for the toilet paper before you get in. It is also recommened to carry a package of tissue in your pocket.**

Transportation

Ulaşım

Turkish road signs conform to the International Road Protocol. Traffic circulates on the right. Speed Limits for cars:

- 50-km/h in urban centers
- 90-km/h in national reoads
- 120-km/h in highways
- 30-km/h in small streets

Public Transport

Toplu Taşıma

Parking is a serious problem in big cities of Turkey. I suggest all visitors to get information about parking before you intend to go any place by your car. Taking a taxi would be more useful in the cities.

Buses

Otobüsler

If you are planning to use public transport, it's more practical to buy a smart ticket, "**Ak-bil**". You can use it either at the bus stops or at the metro stations. There are no discount options for tourists or families.

Dolmuş

It is a special public transport service found only in Turkey. They are collective mini-buses for 10-18 passengers and operating on specific routes. Fares are specified according for the distance traveled and they are relatively cheaper than taxis. The "**Dolmuş**" serves within large cities, to suburbs, airports, and also to neighboring towns.

Taxis

Taksi

Taxis can be found in the streets in big cities and are recognizable by their bright yellow color in Turkey. It is also possible to call from the taxi stations. The fare shown on the taximeter reads according to the distance traveled. From midnight (24:00) to morning (06:00) it will cost 50% more than the daytime fare. In general most taxis do not give receipts. If you need a receipt, please ask the driver if he can give you one before you get on the taxi.

Rent A Car

Araba Kiralama

There are Rent a Car companies if you need a car in Turkey. It is possible to make a reservation before you arrive. You can also get help from the agents of airlines and hotels.

Turkish Airlines (THY)

Türk Hava Yolları

THY have a good security system especially for some countries that have problem with terrorism. Just be more patient, an extra time is need for boarding to the airplane for the security checking's.

WARNINGS:

- **Take care of the opening fares of taximeters for the daytime (gündüz) and for night time (gece) between 12:00 PM and 06:00 AM.**
- **Tipping is not expected unless the driver spends and extra effort for carrying your baggage's and suitcases. You do not have to pay a separate fee for the luggage but a tip is expected if you use the luggage section at the back of the taxi.**
- **Before you decide using a car in Turkey I would like to remind you that Turkish drivers do not obey the traffic rules in general.**

Visa

Vize

The visa situation changes for the citizens of different countries. Citizens of some countries can enter Turkey with a valid passport, a visa is not required for EU countries. It is better to ask for the Turkish Consulate in your country for your country status.

- a valid travel document (Passport except EU countries)
- valid identity is needed (Except EU countries)

Although Turkey is still not an EU country, the entry regulations are set according the customs and entry regulations Turkey has agreed with each individual country.

What To Bring

Ne getirmeli

In summer from June till September:

- light cotton clothes
- a light sweater or jacket (for the evenings)
- a hat
- sun lotions
- sunglasses
- a raincoat (Travelers of Central, Eastern Regions and Northern Region of Anatolia)

In winter and early Spring:

- Winter wear

What To Buy

Ne Almalı

Evil Eye Bead

Nazar boncuğu

The evil eye bead is made of blue glass and will be a very good gift item for your friends. Most people believe that it protects a person from other people's malicious thoughts.

Carpets & Kilims

Halı ve Kilim

Hand-woven Turkish carpets and kilims are worldwide famous. There are many varieties such as material - wool, cotton or silk. The price varies depending on the number of knots per square inch and the material has been used.

Leather Made Goods

Deri Eşya

Turkish leather goods are of very high quality and also cheap.

Textile Goods

Tekstil

Textile goods are clothes, Turkish towels and other all kind of goods made of natural cotton which are very reasonably priced and of high quality.

Jewelery

Mücevherat

Hand made jewelery and the workmanship is wonderful in Turkey. You can find something special at the **Grand Bazaar (Kapalı Çarşı)** in Istanbul as well as other places.

Other goods worth to buy are hand made potteries in areas like **Cappadocia, Pamukkale** etc. You can find vases and many other items made of onyx, tiles, ceramics, and copper.

WARNINGS:

- **Some antiques will be offered you by illegal people and vendors. Do not buy ANTIQUE PIECES they are not allowed to take out of the country!**
- **DRUGS are also illegal and it is a crime with a really heavy punishment.**

Where to Go

Nereye Gitmeli

You can get information about companies who organize **sightseeing tours** from the local tourist offices. They will have details of opening hours and the different excursions available in the area. Hotel personnal can also help you to get in touch with these companies.

Spice Bazaar: Closed on Sundays

Rumeli Fortress: Closed on Wednesdays

Dolmabahce Palace: Closed on Mondays and Thursdays

Museum of Divan Literature (Galata Mevlevihanesi): Closed on Tuesdays

Saint Sophia: Closed on Mondays

Topkapi Palace: Closed on Tuesdays

Kariye Museum: Closed on Wednesdays

Beylerbeyi Palace: Closed on Mondays and Thursdays

Covered Bazaar: Closed on Sundays

Princes Islands

Weights & Measures

Ağırlık ve Uzunluk ölçüleri

Turkey uses the International Metric system.

Weights & Measures	
Weights	**Ağırlıklar**
grams to ounces	**multiply by 0.04**
ounces to grams	**multiply by 28.35**
kilograms to pounds	**multiply by 2.20**
pounds to kilograms	**multiply by 0.45**
Area	**Alan**
1 sq meter	**10.766 ft^2**
Length and Distance	**Uzunluk ve Mesafe**
1 centimeter	**0.3937 inches**
1 meter	**3.280 feet**
1 kilometer	**0.62 miles**
1 meter = 1 kilometer = 0.62 miles	**1.09 yards**
Cubic measurements	**Hacim Ölçüleri**
1 cubic centimeter	**0.06102 in^3**
1 cubic meter	**1.308 yd^3**
1 liter	**0.2643 US gallons**
1 liter	**0.2199 UK gallons**
Temperature	**Isı Ölçüleri**
°C to °F	**multiply by 1.8 and add 32**
°F to °C	**subtract 32, multiply by 5/9**

GLOSSARY

TERİMLER SÖZLÜĞÜ

Glossary Of Business & Economic Terms

İş ve Ekonomik Terimler Sözlüğü

In this section, you will find a glossary of business and economic terms.

INDEX

Subjects	Page
• A	172
• B	174
• C	176
• D	178
• E	179
• F	180
• G	181
• H-I	182
• J-L	184
• M	185
• N-O	186
• P	187
• R	189
• S	191
• T-Z	192

Glossary Of Business & Economic Terms

Iş ve Ekonomik Terimler Sözlüğü

A

abate a tax	**bir vergiyi indirmek**
acceptance against documents	**vesika / belge karşılığı kabul**
accompanied documents	**ilişikteki evraklar**
account	**banka hesabı / kar / hesap**
accountant	**sayman / muhasebeci**
accounting	**muhasebe**
accounts creditors	**alacaklılar hesabı**
accounts department	**muhasebe şubesi**
accrued tax	**tahakkuk etmiş vergi**
acts on documents	**vesika karşılığı avans**
ad campaign (n.)	**reklam kampanyası**
additional income tax	**ek gelir vergisi**
additional tax	**ek vergi / ilave vergi**
address	**adres**
admit to stock exchange	**borsaya kabul edilmek**
advertisement, ad (n.)	**reklam / ilan / poster**
agreement concluded before a notary public	**noterden tasdikli sözleşme**
allocate (v.)	**ayırmak / tahsis etmek/ ödenek ayırmak**
allocation (n.)	**tahsis etme / ayırma / ödenek / dağıtma**
annual net profits	**yıllık net kar**
application documents /papers	**başvuru evrakları**
arbitrage	**arbitraj / tahkim / hakem aracılığı ile bir anlaşmazlığı çözmek**
artisans and small traders	**küçük esnaf ve sanatkar**
assignment	**iş / görev / devir**
assurance	**sigorta / güvence / güven / inanç / cesaret / teminat / söz**
assurance company	**sigorta şirketi**
at a discount	**indirimli / iskontolu**

attesting notary	**tasdik eden noter**
audit department / audit office	**Sayıştay**
audit n.	**denetim / yıllık hesap denetimi**
audit v.	**denetlemek**
auditor (tax)	**vergi denetçisi**

Glossary Of Business & Economic Terms

İş ve Ekonomik Terimler Sözlüğü

B

bad dept	şüpheli alacak
barter (n.)	takas / trampa / mal değiş tokuşu
barter (v.)	takas etmek / takas ticareti ile uğraşmak
barter advertisement	takas ilanı
barter agreement / barter deal	takas anlaşması
barter away	satıp elden çıkarmak / okutmak
barter deal	takas işi
barter economy	takas ekonomisi
barter exchange / barter trade	takas ticareti
barter for	Yahudi pazarlığı yapmak
barter transaction	takas işlemi
barterer	takasçı
bartering	takas ticareti
bartering agreement	takas anlaşması
bartering goods	takas malları
be in debt (v.)	borç içinde olmak / herkese borçlu olmak
be on the board (v.)	(trende, uçakta, otobüste) olmak
before a notary public	noter huzurunda
black market	karaborsa
black marketer	karaborsacı
bond	bono / senet / tahvil
bonded, under bond (customs)	gümrüklenmiş
bookshelf / bookcase	kitaplık
boss	patron
branch	branch
broker market agency	borsa acentası
bulletin board	ilan tahtası
bundle of papers	kâğıt destesi
business	iş / ticaret / meslek / görev
business account	ticari hesap
business administration	işletmecilik / iş idaresi / iş yönetimi

business card / calling card	**kartvizit / kart / ticaret adresi**
business center	**ticaret merkezi / iş merkezi**
business college	**işletmecilik yüksek okulu**
business documents	**iş evrakı**
business expenses	**işletme giderleri**
business papers	**ticari evrak / ticari doküman**
business people	**işadamları**
business relationship	**iş ilişkisi**
business school	**işletmecilik okulu / işletmecilik yüksek okulu**
business suit	**iş davası**
business trip	**iş yolculuğu / iş seyahati**
businesslike (manner)	**sistemli / başarılı**
businessman	**işadamı**
buyer	**alıcı / müşteri**

Glossary Of Business & Economic Terms

İş ve Ekonomik Terimler Sözlüğü

C

cable cordless	**telsiz**
calendar	**takvim / gündem / kayda geçirmek**
call (n.)	**çağrı / davet / kısa ziyaret / uğrama / duyuru / ilan**
call (v.)	**çağırmak / ödemeye davet etmek / uğramak / davet etmek / ilan etmek**
capital	**anapara / sermaye / kapital**
cash	**peşin para / nakit / kasa**
cash (in) (v.)	**paraya çevirmek / nakde çevirmek**
cash discount	**peşin indirimi / nakit iskontosu**
cash dispenser (ATM)	**para çekme makinesi (ATM)**
cash in advance	**peşin**
cashier	**vezne**
cashier (person)	**veznedar / kasiyer**
cashier's check	**kasa çeki / banka çeki**
cell phone	**cep telefonu**
central bank	**merkez bankası**
certified by a notary public	**noter tasdikli / noter onaylı**
certified check	**tasdikli çek**
certified copy	**onaylı kopya / tasdiklenmiş suret**
certify / notarize	**noter tasdiki**
certify notarized copy	**noter tasdikli kopya**
chair	**makam / kürsü**
cipher documents	**şifreli evrak**
claim papers	**dava evrak-ı müsbitesi**
clearance papers	**gümrük ödendiğine dair belgeler**
client	**müşteri / alıcı / müvekkil**
clipboard	**pano**
closing price (stock exchange)	**kapanış fiyatı (borsa)**
commercial papers	**ticari evrak**
commodity market	**mal piyasası / mal borsası / toptan eşya piyasası**
company	**şirket / ortaklık / firma / grup**

compete (v.)	**rekabet etmek / yarışmak**
competition (n.)	**rekabet / yarış**
competitor	**rakip**
concealment of documents	**evrakların hasıraltı edilmesi**
conference	**konferans / müzakere**
conference room	**konferans salonu**
confidential documents	**gizli evrak**
conglomerate	**holding / şirketler topluluğu**
consolidated dept	**konsolide borç**
copier / copy machine	**fotokopi / kopya makinesi**
cord	**kablo / tel**
corporate tax	**kurumlar vergisi**
court papers	**mahkeme dosyaları**
covered	**örtülmüş / sigortalı / kapalı**
covered contract	**sözleşme kapsamı içinde**
covered job	**sosyal sigortalı iş**
covered market	**hal / toptancı hali**
covered option	**teminat maliki**
CPA (certified public accountant)	**yeminli mali müşavir / hesap uzmanı**
credit	**kredi / alacak / itibar**
credit account	**alacaklı hesabı**
credit agreement	**kredi anlaşması**
credit balance	**alacak bakiyesi**
credit card	**kredi kartı**
credit card application	**kredi kartı başvurusu**
credit expense	**kredi giderleri**
credit limit	**kredi limiti**
credit rating	**kredi notu**
creditor	**alacaklı**
currency	**para birimi / para / dolaşma**
currency (exchange) speculation	**döviz spekülasyonu**
currency account	**döviz hesabı**
currency accounting	**para muhasebesi / döviz muhasebesi**
currency agreement	**para anlaşması / döviz sözleşmesi**
currency allowance	**döviz tahsisatı**
currency bill	**döviz senedi**
currency board	**para kurulu**
customer	**müşteri / alıcı**
customer's portfolio	**müşteri portföyü**

Glossary Of Business & Economic Terms

İş ve Ekonomik Terimler Sözlüğü

D

date (n.)	**tarih / randevu tarihi / gün**
date (v.)	**tarih atmak**
debt	**borç yükü**
debt rescheduling	**ödeme planı değişikliği**
debtor	**borçlu / verecekli**
department	**bölüm / kısım / daire / şube**
department manager	**şube müdürü**
depth	**borç yükü / derinlik**
depth of page	**sayfa derinliği**
desk	**yazı masası / büro / daire**
desk knife	**kâğıt açıcı**
desk lamp / desk light	**masa lambası**
desk officer	**yetkili / şube şefi / daire şefi**
desk pad	**sümen**
direct trader	**toptancı tüccar**
discharge papers	**terhis tezkeresi**
discount	**iskonto / indirim / tenzilat / senet kırmak / senet kırdırmak**
discount account	**iskonto hesabı**
discount allowed	**iskonto giderleri / satış iskontosu**
discount allowed to dealer	**bayi iskontosu**
discount basis	**iskonto bazı**
discount bill	**iskonto senedi**
discount broker	**iskonto komisyoncusu / kambiyo tellalı**
discount rate	**indirim oranı / iskonto oranı**
discounts lost	**yararlanılmamış iskonto**
district sales manager	**bölge satış müdürü**
division (section)	**bölüm / şube / bölme işlem (math.)**
division sales manager	**bölüm satış müdürü**
documents	**belgeler / doküman / evrak**
door - to - door trader	**kapı kapı dolaşan satıcı**
drawer (desk)	**çekmece (masa)**
dunning	**uyarı**
dunning letter	**uyarı mektubu (borçlu)**

Glossary Of Business & Economic Terms

İş ve Ekonomik Terimler Sözlüğü

E

economic growth	**ekonomik büyüme / ekonomik kalkınma / iktisadi kalkınma**
economic growth rate	**ekonomik gelişme hızı**
economy	**ekonomi / idare / tasarruf / tutum**
economy campaign / economy drive	**tasarruf kampanyası**
elevator	**asansör**
emergency exit	**acil çıkışı**
employee	**işçi / memur / özlük**
employee appraisal	**personel değerlendirme**
employee benefit paid by company	**sosyal sigorta primi işveren payı**
employee benefits	**sosyal haklar**
employees	**personel / memurlar**
employees' representation	**işçi temsilciliği**
employees' annual report	**yıllık işçi raporu**
employee's association	**işçi derneği**
employee's contribution	**sosyal sigorta primi işçi payı**
employees' layoff	**geçici olarak işten çıkarma**
employee's pension fund	**işçi emeklilik fonu**
employees' representative	**işçi temsilcisi**
employer	**işveren**
enterprise	**girişim / yatırım**
entrance / entry	**giriş**
exchange (stock)	**menkul kıymetler borsası / borsa**
exercise an option	**bir opsiyonu kullanmak**
exit	**çıkış**
expiration date	**vade / sona erme tarihi**
expiry date	**vade / son kullanma tarihi sona erme tarihi**
export sales manager	**ihracat satış müdürü**

Glossary Of Business & Economic Terms

İş ve Ekonomik Terimler Sözlüğü

F

false papers	**sahte evraklar**
fax (n.)	**faks**
fax (v.)	**faks çekmek**
fax machine (n.)	**faks makinesi**
fax number	**faks numarası**
field sales manager	**dış satış müdürü**
file	**dosya / klasör / sicil**
file a bankruptcy petition	**iflas mahkemesine iflasını bildirmek**
file a bill	**dava açmak / dava dilekçesi vermek**
file a claim	**dava açmak**
file a document	**bir evrakı dosyaya kaldırmak**
file a dumping complaint	**damping davası açmak**
file folder	**dosya kapağı / dosya gömleği**
filing cabinet	**dosya dolabı / fiş dolabı / kartoteks**
fine papers	**birinci sınıf senetler**
fire exit	**yangın çıkışı**
firm	**firma / şirket / kuruluş / müessese/ ticarethane**
fiscal year	**mali yıl**
floor	**taban / asgari fiyatlar / zemin / kat**
folder of documents	**kap / evrak dosyası / klasör**
foreign exchange futures market	**vadeli döviz piyasası**
forward interest rate	**vadeli faiz oranı**
futures market	**vadeli piyasalar / vadeli işlem piyasası**

Glossary Of Business & Economic Terms

İş ve Ekonomik Terimler Sözlüğü

G

gamble on the stock exchange	**borsada spekülasyon yapmak**
general manager	**genel müdür / umum müdür**
general sales manager	**genel satış müdürü**
global economy	**küresel ekonomi**
global trade	**küresel ticaret**
globalization (n.)	**küreselleşme**
glue	**tutkal / zamk / yapıştırıcı**
government bonds	**devlet tahvili**
gross (n.)	**brüt / hepsi / bütün**
gross assets	**brüt aktif / bir şirketin tüm varlığı**
gross domestic product	**gayrı safi yurtiçi gelir**
gross income	**brüt gelir / vergi öncesi gelir**
gross national product (GNP)	**gayri safi milli hasıla / gayrı safi milli gelir**
gross profit	**brüt kar / gayrı safi kar**
gross turnover	**brüt ciro**
gross weight	**brüt ağırlık**

Glossary Of Business & Economic Terms

Iş ve Ekonomik Terimler Sözlüğü

H - I

hall	**toplantı salonu / giriş / hol**
hawker	**seyyar satıcı**
hole punch	**delikli zımba**
home sales manager	**memleket içi satış müdürü**
in depth	**enine boyuna etraflıca**
industrial accident	**iş kazası**
industry	**sanayi / endüstri / çalışkanlık / meşguliyet**
industry association	**sanayiciler derneği**
industry complex	**sanayi kompleksi / endüstri kompleksi**
industry contractor	**endüstri müteahhidi**
industry development	**sınai kalkınma**
industry executives	**sanayi yönetici kadrosu**
industry figures	**sanayi rakamları**
industry group	**sanayi grubu**
industrial growth	**sınai gelişim**
industry leader	**lider sanayici**
ink	**mürekkep**
insurance	**sigorta / sigorta taksidi**
insurance against accident	**kaza sigortası**
insurance against all risks	**genel risk sigortası**
insurance against damage	**hasar sigortası**
insturance against damage coused by natural forces	**doğal afet sigortası**
insturance against damage property	**hasar sigortası**
insurance against loss of use	**iş kaybı sigortası**
insurance agency	**sigorta acentası**
insurance agent	**sigorta ajanı**
insurance application	**sigorta başvurusu**
insurance appraisal	**hasar takdiri / hasar değerlendirilmesi**
insurance appraiser	**sigorta eksperi**
insurance auditor	**sigorta denetçisi**

insurance bank	**sigorta kurumu**
insurance premium	**sigorta primi / sigorta ücreti**
interest	**faiz**
interest bearing	**faiz getiren**
interest rates	**faiz oranı / faiz haddi**
investment	**yatırım / para koyma**
investment account	**yatırım hesabı**
investment accounting	**yatırım muhasebesi**
investment activities	**yatırım faaliyetleri**
investment aid	**yatırım yardımı**
investment allowance	**yatırım muafiyeti**
investor	**yatırımcı**
invoice	**fatura**
invoice amount	**fatura bedeli**
invoice book	**fatura defteri**
invoice cost	**fatura maliyeti**
invoice date	**fatura tarihi**
invoice number	**fatura numarası**
invoice supervision	**fatura kontrolü**
invoice total	**fatura tutarı**

Glossary Of Business & Economic Terms

İş ve Ekonomik Terimler Sözlüğü

J - L

job	**iş / meslek / görev**
key	**anahtar / tuş / şifre / klavye**
keyboard	**klavye**
know-how	**teknik bilgi**
labor	**işçi / işçi sınıfı**
labor contract	**iş sözleşmesi**
labor cost	**emek maliyeti / işçilik**
labor court	**iş mahkemesi**
labor dispute	**iş anlaşmazlığı**
labor force	**işgücü**
labor intensive	**emek - yoğun teknoloji**
labor law	**iş kanunu**
labor placement office	**iş ve işçi bulma kurumu**
labor recruitment	**işçi alma**
labor report	**çalışma raporu / iş raporu**
labor supply	**emek arzı**
labor theory of value	**emek değer teorisi**
large- lot trader	**toplu alım satım yapan borsa tüccarı**
launch v.	**iş başlatmak**
letter	**mektup / harf**
letter of credit	**kredi mektubu**
letter opener	**mektup açacağı**
letters credentials	**güven mektubu / itimatname**
letters of business	**iş ruhsatı**
letters of caption	**tutuklama emri**
letters of commendation	**tavsiye mektubu**
letters of guarantee	**garanti mektupları**
life insurance	**hayat sigortası**
lift	**asansör**

Glossary Of Business & Economic Terms

İş ve Ekonomik Terimler Sözlüğü

M

manager	**yönetici / idareci / müdür**
market	**piyasa / pazar / çarşı**
market analysis	**piyasa analizi / pazar analizi**
market area	**pazar / pazar alanı**
market assessment	**piyasa değerlendirmesi**
market assumption	**piyasayı ele geçirme**
market audit	**piyasa etüdü / piyasa araştırması**

Glossary Of Business & Economic Terms

İş ve Ekonomik Terimler Sözlüğü

N - O

national debt	**devlet borcu / milli borç**
national	**milli ulusal**
national accounting	**milli muhasebe**
national - production index	**milli üretim endeksi**
net	**net / saf / kesintisiz**
net assets	**net aktifler / net varlıklar**
net income	**net kar / net gelir**
net income after taxes	**vergi düşülmüş net gelir**
net profits	**net kar**
notarized copy	**noter tasdikli kopya**
notary fee	**noter harcı**
notary public	**noter**
notary public's clerk	**noter kâtibi**
notary's clerk	**noter memuru**
notary's office	**noterlik / noter bürosu**
notebook	**defter / not defteri**
notice	**uyarı / ihbar / bildiri / tebliğ / ilan**
notice board	**ilan tahtası**
office	**ofis / yazıhane / büro / daire / işyeri / bölüm**
office supplies	**büro malzemeleri**
on credit	**veresiye**
option	**seçenek / seçim / vade / tercih / şık**

Glossary Of Business & Economic Terms

İş ve Ekonomik Terimler Sözlüğü

P

paper	kâğıt / senet / belge / vesika / araştırma / bildiri / gazete
papers	evrak / vesaik
papers and periodicals	gazeteler ve dergiler
papers with various periods to run	muhtelif vadeleri olan senetler
partition	bölüm / taksim / kısım / parça / tahta perde / duvar
pen	dolmakalem / tükenmez kalem
pencil	kurşun kalem
pencil sharpener	kalemtıraş
per capita net income	kişi başına düşen net gelir
petty cash	küçük kasa / küçük kasa hesabı
petty trader	küçük tüccar
photocopy	fotokopi makinesi
pin	toplu iğne
portfolio	evrak çantası / portföy / cüzdan / bir kimsenin toplam tahvilleri
portfolio accounts	portföy hesapları
portfolio buying	portföy alışları
portfolio changes	portföy değişiklikleri
portfolio investment	portföy yatırımı
portfolio management	portföy yönetimi
portfolio manager	portföy yöneticisi
portfolio of shares	hisse senetleri portföyü
postage stamp	posta pulu
premium	prim / ikramiye / hediye / sigorta ücreti / değer / ödül
price	fiyat / eder / paha / değer / kıymet / rüşvet
printer	yazıcı
profit	kar / kazanç / yarar / menfaat / fayda / kar getirmek / kazanmak / çıkar/ semere

profit-bearing	**kar getiren**
profit-earning capacity	**karlılık**
profits of business	**işletme karı**
profits rise	**kar artışı**
profit-sharing bonds	**kar paylı tahviller**
proper money	**merkez bankası parası**
provisional tax return	**geçici vergi beyannamesi**
pull (door etc.) (v.)	**çek (kapı vs.)**
purchase (n.)	**satın alma / alış / alım / satın alınan şey**
purchase (purchasing) permit	**satın alma izni**
purchase (v.)	**satın almak**
purchase agreement	**satın alma sözleşmesi**
purchase at auction	**açık artırmada almak**
purchase at first hand	**ilk elden satın almak**
purchase at option	**opsiyonlu alım**
purchase book	**alış defteri**
purchase budget	**satın alma bütçesi**
purchase commitment	**alış taahhüdü**
purchase contract	**satın alma sözleşmesi**
purchase costs	**satın alma giderleri**
purchase order	**alım emri / satın alma emri**
purchaser	**alıcı / müşteri**
purchases account	**alış hesabı**
purchases discount	**alış iskontosu**
purchases journal	**günlük alış defteri**
push (door etc.) (v.)	**it (kapı vs.)**

Glossary Of Business & Economic Terms

İş ve Ekonomik Terimler Sözlüğü

R

receipt	alındı / makbuz / satış fişi / fiş
receipt book	alındı defteri / makbuz defteri
receipt for goods	mal teslim belgesi
receipt for loan	ödünç makbuzu
receipt for payment	ödeme makbuzu
receipt for rent	kira makbuzu
receipt for the balance	bakiye makbuzu
receipt form	alındı kâğıdı / makbuz
receipt given	kesilen makbuz
receipt holder	makbuz hamili
receipt in blank	boş makbuz
receipts and expenses	gelir - gider
receipts and payments	tahsilat ve ödemeler
receipts of the day	günlük tahsilat
reception	resepsiyon / karşılama / kabul
receptionist	resepsiyon / resepsiyon görevlisi / resepsiyon memuru
renewal papers (insurance)	yenileme evrakı
report (n.)	rapor / zabıt / bildirge / denetçi raporu / söylenti / bilgi / haber
report (v.)	haber vermek / yaymak / ihbar etmek / anlatmak / resmen bildirmek / rapor vermek / yazmak
risk	tehlike / tehlikeye sokmak / risk / riziko
risk adjusted discount rate	riske ayarlı iskonto oranı
risk analysis	risk analizi
risk appraisal	risk değerlendirilmesi
risk assessment	risk tespiti
risk assets	riskli aktif değerler
risk assumption	risk üstlenme
risk assurance	risk sigortası
risk averse	riskten kaçınan

risk aversion	**riskten kaçınma**
risk avoidance	**riske karşı alınan önlemler**
risk bearer	**risk konusu / risk hamili**
risk benefit ratio	**risk kazanç oranı**
risk capital	**risk sermayesi**
risk management	**risk yönetimi**
risks assured by the buyer	**risklerin alıcı tarafından yüklenilmesi**
risks of carriage	**taşıma riski / nakliyat riski**
ruler	**cetvel**

Glossary Of Business & Economic Terms

İş ve Ekonomik Terimler Sözlüğü

S

safe and sound	**sağ salim**
safe arrival	**sağ salim varış**
safe bill	**sağlam senet**
safe breaker	**kasa hırsızı**
safe builder	**kasa yapımcısı**
safe buster	**kasa açıcısı**
safe conduct	**geçiş tezkeresi**
safe (n.)	**güvenilir / emin / sağlam / güvenli**
safe-deposit box	**kiralık kasa**
sales manager	**satış müdürü**
scissors	**makas**
second hand	**ikinci el**
secondary (adj.)	**ikincil / tali / sonraki**
secretary	**sekreter**
speculation	**vurgun / borsa oyunu / spekülasyon / vurgunculuk / kurgu**
speculator	**spekülatör / vurguncu**
stair	**basamak / kademe / merdiven**
stairwell	**merdiven boşluğu**
staple (for stapler)	**zımba teli**
stapler	**tel zımba**
stationery	**kırtasiye**
stock (n.)	**hisse senedi / stok**
stock (v.)	**stok yapmak / mal yığmak**
stock exchange	**menkul kıymetler borsası / borsa**
stock exchange index	**borsa endeksi**
stock exchange market	**hisse senedi ve tahvil piyasası**
stock market turnover	**borsa cirosu**
stock - exchange agent	**borsa ajanı**
stock - exchange creditor	**borsa alacaklısı**
subsidiary	**bayi / yan kuruluş / şube / tali**
suggestion box	**şikayet kutusu / öneri kutusu**
supplies	**malzeme / gereçler / erzak mal**

Glossary Of Business & Economic Terms

İş ve Ekonomik Terimler Sözlüğü

T - Z

Institute for Standardization Of Turkey (TSE)	**Türk Standartlar Enstitüsü (TSE)**
tax (n.)	**vergi / resim / külfet**
tax (v.)	**vergilendirmek / vergi yüklemek / zorlamak**
tax assessment	**vergi matrahı**
tax audit (n.)	**vergi denetimi**
tax collector	**vergi tahsildarı**
tax consultant	**vergi danışmanı / vergi müşaviri**
tax evasion	**vergi kaçırma / vergi kaçakçılığı**
tax return	**vergi beyannamesi**
taxpayer	**vergi yükümlüsü / vergi mükellefi**
ticker (US)	**borsa komisyoncusu**
title	**başlık / unvan**
title (person)	**isim**
total net income	**toplam net gelir**
trade (n.)	**ticaret / alışveriş / iş / pazarlık / tüccarlık / alım satım**
trade (v.)	**ticaret yapmak / alışveriş yapmak**
trade fair	**ticaret fuarı**
trade- journal	**ticaret gazetesi**
trade paper	**ticaret senedi / ticaret gazetesi**
trade union	**işçi sendikası / sendika**
trade union contributions	**sendika aidatı**
trade union leader	**sendika başkanı**
trade union legislation	**sendikacılık mevzuatı**
trader	**tacir tüccar**
trades	**esnaf**
trading	**alışveriş / ticaret / değiş tokuş/ iş hacmi / muamele**
trading ability	**ticari beceri / satış kabiliyeti**
trading account	**işletme hesabı / ticaret hesabı**
trading accounts	**ticari muhasebe defterleri**

trading activity	**ticari faaliyet**
trading advantage	**ticari üstünlük / avantaj**
trading area	**ticaret alanı / iş alanı**
trading arrangement	**ticaret anlaşması**
trading loss	**ticari zarar**
trading partner	**şirket ortağı / ticari ortak**
transaction	**işlem / hareket / muamele / iş görme**
transaction cost	**işlem maliyeti**
transaction date	**işlem tarihi**
transaction for future delivery	**vadeli işlem**
transactions	**hesap özeti**
transactions in gold	**altın ticareti**
transactions tax	**muamele vergisi**
type (v.)	**daktilo ile yazmak**
typing error (n.)	**daktilo hatası**
value	**kıymet / değer / önem / itibar / değer biçmek / kıymet takdir etmek**
value added	**katma değer**
value added tax (VAT)	**katma değer vergisi (KDV)**
value added tax exempt	**(KDV) katma değer vergisinden muaf**
venture capital (n.)	**risk sermayesi**
volatility	**oynaklık / kararsızlık**
waste paper basket	**çöp sepeti**
welfare	**sosyal yardım**

Glossary Of Computers & Internet Terms

Bilgisayar ve İnternet Terimleri Sözlüğü

In this section, you will find a glossary of business and economic terms.

INDEX

Subjects	Page
• A-B	195
• C	196
• D	198
• E	200
• F	201
• G-I	202
• J-L	204
• M	206
• N-O	208
• P	210
• R	212
• S	214
• T-U	216
• V-Z	217

Computers & Internet

Bilgisayar ve İnternet Terimleri

A - B

accept (v.)	**onaylamak / kabul etmek**
accept	**onayla / kabul et**
accessibility	**erişilirlik**
accuracy	**doğruluk**
acronym	**kısa ad**
action bar	**menü çubuğu**
activate (program etc.) (v.)	**etkinleştirmek**
adapter	**bağdaştırıcı**
add (v.)	**ekle**
approve(v.)	**onaylamak**
archive	**belgelik / arşiv**
area	**alan**
arrow	**ok**
arrow key	**ok tuşu**
attachment	**ek**
back (v.)	**geri dön**
background	**artalan**
backup (n.)	**yedekleme**
backup (v.)	**yedeklemek**
back tab	**geri sekme**
banner	**büyük başlık**
bar	**çubuk**
battery	**pil**
black-and-white	**siyah - beyaz**
blank	**boş / boşluk**
bookmark (v.)	**işaretle**
box	**kutu**
browse (v.)	**göz atmak**
bug	**yanlış**

Computers & Internet

Bilgisayar ve İnternet Terimleri

C

cable	**kablo**
cache	**önbellek**
cancel	**iptal et / vazgeç**
cancel (v.)	**vazgeçmek**
capital letter	**büyük harf**
caps lock	**büyük harf kilidi**
case sensitive	**büyük ve küçük harf duyarlı**
CD-Rom	**CD-Rom**
CD-Rom driver	**CD-Rom sürücü**
CD-Rom player	**CD-Rom okuyucu**
click (on) (v.)	**tıkla**
clipboard	**pano / taşıma panosu**
clock	**saat**
clockwise	**saat yönü**
close (v.)	**kapatmak**
close	**kapat**
command	**komut**
compact disc	**CD / optik disk**
compute	**hesaplamak**
computer	**bilgisayar**
computer aided design	**bilgisayar destekli tasarım (BDT)**
computer aided education	**bilgisayar destekli eğitim (BDT)**
computer science	**bilgisayar bilimleri**
confirm	**doğrula /onayla**
confirm (v.)	**onaylamak**
connect	**bağlan**
connect (v.)	**bağlanmak**
connection	**bağlantı**
continue	**sürdür / devam et**
continue (v.)	**devam etmek / sürdürmek**
control (v.)	**denetlemek / kontrol etmek**
control menu	**denetim menüsü**
control panel	**denetim masası**

controller	**denetleyici**
copy (v.)	**kopyalamak**
copy	**kopyala**
copy (n.)	**kopya**
counter	**sayaç / karşı**
counter clockwise	**saat yönünün tersi**
cover (on a device) (n.)	**örtü**
cross reference	**çapraz başvuru**
cursor	**imleç**
customizable	**(isteğe göre) uyarlanır**
customize (v.)	**(isteğe göre) uyarlamak**
cut (v.)	**kesmek**
cut	**kes**
cut and paste	**kes ve yapıştır**

Computers & Internet

Bilgisayar ve İnternet Terimleri

D

damage	**zarar vermek**
data	**veri**
database	**veri tabanı**
default	**varsayılan**
delete	**sil / iptal et**
delete key	**sil tuşu**
desktop	**masaüstü**
device	**aygıt**
digital	**sayısal**
directory	**dizin / rehber**
disk	**disk**
disk array	**disk dizisi**
disk drive	**disk sürücü**
disk error	**disk hatası**
disk space	**disk alanı**
diskette (n.)	**disket**
display (v.)	**görüntülemek**
domain	**etki alanı**
done	**bitti**
double click	**çift tıklama**
double-click (on) (v.)	**çift tıkla**
down	**aşağı / bozuk**
down arrow	**aşağı ok**
down time	**bozuk kalma süresi**
download (v.)	**yüklemek**
draft	**taslak**
drag (v.)	**sürüklemek**
drag	**sürükle**
draw (v.)	**çizmek**
drawer	**çekmece**
drawing	**çizim**
drive (v.)	**sürmek**
driver (n.)	**sürücü**

duplicate (v.)	**çoğaltmak**
duplication	**çoğaltma**
duplicator	**çoğaltıcı**
duration	**süre**
dust cover (n.)	**koruyucu örtü**

Computers & Internet

Bilgisayar ve İnternet Terimleri

E

edge	**kenar**
edit	**düzenlemek**
edition	**basım**
editor	**düzenleyici**
encrypt	**şifrelemek**
end (v.)	**bitirmek**
end key	**bitir tuşu**
enlarge (v.)	**büyütmek**
enter (v.)	**girmek**
enter key	**gir tuşu**
entry	**giriş**
error	**hata**
error message	**hata iletisi**
esc key / escaping key	**esc tuşu / kaçış tuşu**
Ethernet	**Eternet**
exit (v.)	**çıkmak**
export (n.)	**dışarı aktarım**
export (v.)	**dışarı aktarmak**
extension	**uzantı (dosya adları)**
extension cord	**uzatma kablosu**
external	**dış**
external modem	**dış modem**
extract (v.)	**seçip çıkartmak**

Computers & Internet

Bilgisayar ve İnternet Terimleri

F

facility	**olanak**
fail (v.)	**başarısız olmak**
false	**yanlış / hata**
fatal error	**onulmaz yanlış**
fault	**aksaklık**
feed	**besleme**
feedback	**geribildirim**
field	**alan**
file	**dosya**
fill	**doldurma**
filter	**süzgeç / süzmek**
final	**son**
find	**bulma / bul**
find and replace	**bul ve değiştir**
finish (v.)	**bitirmek**
flag (noun)	**bayrak**
flash	**yanıp sönmek**
floating	**kayan**
floppy disk	**disket**
floppy disk drive	**disket sürücü**
flow	**akış / akmak**
flowchart	**akış çizelgesi**
folder	**klasör**
form	**form / biçim**
format	**biçim / biçimlemek**
forward	**ileri / ileriye**
free	**boş**
free memory	**boş bellek**
full screen	**tüm ekran / tam ekran**

Computers & Internet

Bilgisayar ve İnternet Terimleri

G - I

go to	**git**
graphic	**grafik**
guidance	**yol gösterme**
guide	**kılavuz**
guideline	**yönerge**
gutter	**cilt payı**
hard copy	**basılı kopya**
hard disk	**disk / hafıza**
hardware	**donanım**
height	**yükseklik**
help (n.)	**yardım**
help desk	**yardım masası**
help index	**yardım dizini**
hide (v.)	**gizlemek**
highlight (to) (v.)	**vurgulamak**
home directory	**ana dizin**
home page	**ana sayfa**
horizontal	**yatay**
icon	**simge / sembol**
ID number	**kimlik numarası**
ignore (v.)	**yoksaymak**
image	**görüntü**
import (v.)	**içeri aktarmak**
important	**önemli**
improved	**iyileştirilmiş**
in use light	**kullanımda ışığı**
inactive	**etkin olmayan**
in-basket	**gelen sepeti**
inbox	**gelen kutusu**
include	**içermek**
incoming	**gelen**
increase	**artırmak**
index	**dizin**

indicate (v.)	**göstermek**
indicator	**gösterge**
indirect	**dolaylı**
info / information	**bilgi**
information technology (IT)	**bilişim teknolojisi**
initial	**başlangıç / ilk**
initialize	**başlangıç durumuna getirmek / sıfırlamak**
initialize (v.)	**kişiselleştir**
initials	**baş harfler (bir ismin)**
input	**girdi / giriş**
input device	**giriş aygıtı**
input/output	**giriş / çıkış**
inquiry	**sorgu**
insert (v.)	**araya eklemek**
insert (floppy disk etc.) (v.)	**(disketi) takmak**
install (v.)	**kurmak / yüklemek**
instruction	**komut / yönerge**
internet	**internet**
interrupt (v.)	**kesmek**
interrupt (n.)	**kesme / kesinti**
introduction	**giriş**
invalid	**geçersiz**
invisible	**görünmeyen**
ISP, internet service provider	**internet servis sağlayıcı**
italic	**italik**
item	**öğe**

Computers & Internet

Bilgisayar ve İnternet Terimleri

J - L

join (v.)	**birleştirmek**
justify	**yaslamak**
key (n.) [on keyboard]	**anahtar / tuş**
keyboard	**klavye**
key pad	**tuş takımı**
keystroke (v.)	**tuşa basmak**
keyword	**anahtar sözcük**
Kilobyte (KB)	**Kilobyte (KB)**
label	**etiket**
LAN (local area network)	**yerel ağ**
language	**dil**
laptop computer	**dizüstü bilgisayar**
lasso	**kement**
last	**son**
layer	**katman**
left adjust	**sola yaslamak**
left aligned	**sola yaslanmış**
left alignment	**sola yaslama**
left justify (v.)	**sola yaslamak**
letter	**harf / mektup**
library	**kitaplık**
license	**lisans / izin**
light	**ışık**
limit	**sınır**
line	**çizgi / satır / hat**
link (v.)	**bağlamak**
link (to)	**bağlan**
list	**liste**
list (v.)	**listelemek**
load (v.)	**yüklemek**
local	**yerel**
locate (v.)	**yerini belirlemek**
location	**yer**

lock	**kilit**
lock (v.)	**kilitlemek**
log in/on (v.)	**oturum açmak / bağlanmak**
log out/off (v.)	**oturum kapamak**
login	**oturum açmak**
logo	**logo / amblem**
lookup	**arama**
lowercase	**küçük harf**

Computers & Internet

Bilgisayar ve İnternet Terimleri

M

macro	**makro**
main	**ana**
main memory / main storage	**ana bellek**
manual	**el ile / elkitabı**
map	**eşlemek**
margin	**kenar boşluğu**
mark (n)	**im / işaret**
mark (v)	**imlemek / işaretlemek**
master	**ana**
master copy	**ana kopya**
match	**eşleştirmek**
maximize	**ekranı kaplamak**
maximum	**en büyük / en çok**
mean	**ortalama**
measurement	**ölçüm**
medium	**ortam / orta**
Megabyte (measurement unit)	**Megabyte, MB**
Megahertz	**Megahertz**
member	**üye**
memory (ram)	**hafıza / bellek**
menu (computer)	**menü**
menu bar	**menü çubuğu**
merge	**birleştirmek**
message	**ileti / mesaj**
method	**yöntem**
minimize	**simge durumuna küçültmek**
minimum	**en küçük / en az**
minor	**küçük / önemsiz**
minus	**eksi**
mirroring	**ikizleme**
missing	**eksik / atlanmış**
misspelling	**yazım hatası**
mixed	**karma**

mode	**kip**
model	**model**
modem	**modem**
modification	**değişiklik**
modify (v.)	**değiştirmek**
monitor (n.)	**monitör / görüntü birimi**
mouse (mice)	**fare**
mouse button	**fare düğmesi**
mouse pad	**fare altlığı**
mouse pointer	**fare imleci**
move (v.)	**taşımak**
move	**taşı**
multimedia	**çoklu ortam**
multiply	**çarpmak**
mutual	**karşılıklı**
mutually exclusive	**birbirini dışlayan**

Computers & Internet

Bilgisayar ve İnternet Terimleri

N - O

name	**ad**
national language character set	**ulusal dil karakter kümesi**
national language support	**ulusal dil desteği**
native	**yerel**
navigation	**dolaşma**
network (n.)	**ağ**
networking	**ağ oluşturma**
new	**yeni**
next	**sonraki**
next - previous	**ileri - geri**
nickname	**takma ad**
none	**hiçbiri**
notice (v.)	**bildirmek**
notify (v.)	**bildirmek**
number	**sayı**
object	**nesne**
odd	**tek**
off	**kapalı**
office	**ofis**
off - line	**çevrimdışı**
ok	**tamam**
ok done	**tamam uygula**
omit (v.)	**atlamak**
on	**açık**
on-line	**çevrimiçi**
opacity	**ışık geçirmezlik**
open (n.)	**açık**
open (v.)	**açmak**
open	**aç**
operate (v.)	**işletmek**
operating system	**işletim sistemi**
operation	**işlem**
operator	**işletmen / operatör**

optimization	**eniyileme**
optimum	**en iyi**
option	**seçenek**
optional	**seçmeli**
order (n.)	**komut / sipariş**
order (v.)	**düzenlemek**
organize (v.)	**düzenlemek**
original	**özgün / orijinal**
outlet	**çıkış noktası**
outline	**ana çizgiler / çerçeve**
outline (font)	**dış çizgi**
outlook	**görünüm**
out-of-memory	**yetersiz bellek**
output	**çıktı / çıkış**
output device	**çıkış aygıtı**
overlay	**yer paylaşmak**
overview	**gözden geçirmek**
overwrite	**üstüne yazmak**
owner	**sahip**
owners guide	**kullanıcı kılavuzu**

Computers & Internet

Bilgisayar ve İnternet Terimleri

P

pack (v.)	**paketlemek / sıkıştırmak**
package	**paket**
page	**sayfa**
page break	**sayfa sonu**
page down	**sonraki sayfa**
page layout	**sayfa düzeni**
page number	**sayfa numarası**
page printer	**sayfa yazıcı**
page setup	**sayfa düzeni**
page up	**önceki sayfa**
panel	**pano / panel**
paragraph	**paragraf**
parent	**üst**
parent directory	**üst dizin**
password	**parola / şifre**
password protection	**şifre koruması**
paste (v.)	**yapıştırmak**
patch (v.)	**yamamak**
path	**yol**
pattern	**örüntü / desen**
pause (v.)	**duraklamak**
perform (v.)	**gerçekleştirmek**
personal computer	**kişisel bilgisayar**
phase	**evre**
plain text	**düz metin**
plug	**fiş**
point	**nokta / göstermek**
point (measure)	**punto**
pop up menu	**açılır menü**
pop up message	**beliren ileti**
pop up window	**açılır pencere**
position	**konum**
positive	**olumlu / artı**

postpone (v.)	**ertelemek**
power	**güç**
power (on/off) button	**açma / kapama düğmesi**
power off	**kapamak**
power on	**açmak**
preface	**önsöz**
preferences	**tercihler / yeğlenenler**
press (v.)	**basmak**
press (key) (v.)	**dokun**
preview	**önizleme**
previous	**önceki**
previous - next	**geri - ileri**
previous settings	**önceki ayarlar**
primary	**birincil**
print (v.)	**yazmak / yazdırmak**
print cartridge	**yazıcı kartuşu**
print head	**yazıcı kafası**
printer	**yazıcı**
program (n.)	**program**
program (v.)	**programlamak**
properties	**özellikler**
provider (ISP)	**sağlayıcı**
purge	**temizlemek**

Computers & Internet

Bilgisayar ve İnternet Terimleri

R

raise (v.)	yükseltmek
ram (memory)	hafıza
random	rastgele
recall	geri çağırmak
receipt	alındı
receive (v.)	almak
receiver	alıcı
recent	en son
record (n.)	kayıt
record (v.)	kaydetmek
recover (v.)	kurtarmak
recoverable	kurtarılır
recovery	kurtarma
recycle (v.)	yeniden çevrime sokmak
reduce (v.)	küçültmek
reminder	anımsatıcı / hatırlatıcı
remove (v.)	kaldırmak / çıkarmak
rename (v.)	yeniden adlandırmak
repair	onarım
repeat (v.)	yinelemek
replace (v.)	yerine koymak / değiştirmek
reply	yanıt
request	istek
requirement	gereksinim
reset (v.)	ilk duruma getirmek / sıfırlamak
resize (v.)	yeniden boyutlandırmak
resolution	çözünürlük
restart (v.)	yeniden başlatmak
restart	yeniden başlat
restore (v.)	geri yüklemek
retry (v.)	yeniden denemek
return (v.)	dönmek
return key	geri dönüş tuşu

root directory	**kök dizin**
rotate (v.)	**döndürmek**
round (v.)	**yuvarlamak**
router	**yöneltici**
row	**sıra / dizi**
royalty	**telif hakkı**
rule	**kural**
ruler	**cetvel**
run (v.)	**çalıştırmak**

S

save (v.)	**saklamak**
save	**sakla / koru**
save as	**yeni adla kaydet**
scanner	**tarayıcı**
screen	**ekran**
screen saver	**ekran koruyucu**
scroll (v.)	**kaydırmak**
search	**ara**
search (v.)	**aramak**
search and replace	**bul ve değiştir**
search direction	**arama yönü**
search engine	**arama motoru**
search path	**arama yolu**
select	**seç**
select (v.)	**seçmek**
select all	**tümünü seç**
send (v.)	**göndermek**
send	**gönder**
separator	**ayırıcı**
server	**sunucu**
service	**hizmet**
set (n.)	**küme / takım**
set (v.)	**belirlemek / ayarlamak**
settings	**ayarlar**
setup (n.)	**düzenek**
setup (v.)	**kurmak / hazırlamak**
shift (v.)	**ötelemek / kaydırmak**
shift key	**üst karakter tuşu**
short	**kısa**
shortcut	**kısayol**
shortcut key	**kısayol tuşu**
show (v.)	**göstermek**
shut down (v.) (computer etc.)	**kapat** (bilgisayar vs.)

sift (v.)	**elemek**
signal	**işaret**
signature	**imza**
sign-off	**oturumu kapamak**
sign-on	**oturumu açmak**
sleeping mode	**uyku durumu**
slice	**dilim**
slow	**yavaş**
software (n.)	**yazılım**
sort (v.)	**sıralamak**
sort	**sırala**
space	**boşluk / alan**
space key	**boşluk tuşu**
speaker	**hoparlör**
special character	**özel karakterler**
speed	**hız**
spell checking (n.)	**yazım denetimi**
start (program)	**başla**
start (v.)	**başlamak**
status bar	**durum çubuğu**
step	**adım**
stop (v.)	**durmak / durdurmak**
store	**depolamak**
stream	**akım**
streaming	**duraksız işlem / akıcı**
streaming mode	**duraksız kip**
strikeout (v.)	**çıkartmak**
style	**biçim / stil**
sub	**alt**
subdirectory	**altdizin**
subject (n.)	**konu**
suggest (to) (v.)	**önermek**
suggestion	**öneri**
summary	**özet**
switch	**anahtar**
switch off (v.)	**kapamak**
switch on (v.)	**açmak**

Computers & Internet

Bilgisayar ve İnternet Terimleri

T - U

tab (n.)	**sekme**
table	**çizelge / tablo**
timeout	**zaman aşımı**
timer	**süre ölçer**
tip	**ipucu / fiş ucu**
title	**başlık**
toolbar	**araç çubuğu**
toolbox	**araç kutusu**
toolkit	**araç takımı**
top	**üst**
top margin	**üst kenar boşluğu**
top of page	**sayfa başı**
transfer (v.)	**aktarmak / aktarım**
transfer	**aktar**
transfer rate	**aktarım hızı**
transform	**dönüştürmek / dönüşüm**
trash	**çöp sepeti**
tray	**tepsi**
troubleshoot	**düzeltici**
troubleshooting	**sorun giderme**
tune	**ayar**
tuner	**ayarlayıcı**
turn off	**kapat**
turn on	**aç**
undo	**geri almak**
upload (v.)	**(yukarı) yüklemek**
update (v.)	**güncellemek**
user	**kullanıcı**
user ID	**kullanıcı kimliği**
user's guide	**kullanıcı kılavuzu**
user's reference	**başvuru kitabı**

Computers & Internet

Bilgisayar ve İnternet Terimleri

V - Z

valid	**geçerli**
validate (v.)	**geçerliğini denetlemek**
verification	**doğrulama**
verify (v.)	**doğruluğunu sağlamak**
version	**sürüm, uyarlama**
vertical	**düşey**
view (n.)	**görünüm / görüntüleme**
view (v.)	**seyret / bak**
virus	**virüs**
visual	**görsel**
wait (v.)	**beklemek**
warning	**uyarı**
warning beep	**uyarı sesi**
warning message	**uyarı iletisi**
web (www)	**ağ**
web page	**veb sayfası**
website	**veb sitesi**
width	**genişlik / en**
window	**pencere**
word	**sözcük**
word processing	**sözcük işlem**
word wrap	**sözcük kaydırma**
worksheet	**taslak / işlem tablosu**
zone	**bölge**
zoom in	**yaklaştırmak / büyütmek**
zoom out	**uzaklaştırmak / küçültmek**

E-Mail Terms

E-Posta Terimleri

address book	**adres defteri**
"at" sign, @	**et işareti**
address (n.)	**adres**
answer (n.)	**cevap**
attached	**eklendi**
attachment	**ek**
check e-mails	**mektupları kontrol et**
compose (a new message)	**(yeni mesaj) hazırla**
download (n.)	**yükleme**
download (v.) (e-mail)	**(e-mail) yükle**
draft (e-mail) (n.)	**taslak**
e-mail	**elektronik posta**
e-mail message (n.)	**e-mesaj**
e-mail box (n.)	**e-posta kutusu**
in-box (n.)	**gelen kutusu**
junk mail (n.)	**reklam vs. ıvır zıvır posta**
mail (n.)	**posta**
mail (v.)	**postalamak**
mailbox (n.)	**posta kutusu / mektup kutsu**
mailing (n.)	**postalama**
mailing address	**e-posta adresi**
mailing list	**posta listesi**
new message (n.)	**yeni mesaj**
nickname	**takma ad**
out-box (n.)	**giden kutusu**
outgoing	**giden**
password	**şifre**
password protected	**şifre korumalı**
reply (n.)	**cevap**
reply	**cevapla**
reply (v.)	**Cevap vermek**
send e-mail (v.)	**mesaj gönder**
sender	**gönderen / gönderici**
spell-check (n.)	**yazım kontrolü**

subject (n.)	**konu**
unread	**okunmamış**
unread messages	**okunmamış mesajlar**

Nationalities

Milliyetler Sözlüğü

Plural forms of nouns are formed by the suffixes **-ler** or **-lar**. In order to choose which suffix will be added to a noun look at the last syllable of the noun. If the vowel of the last syllable is one of **i, e, ö, ü** use **-ler**, otherwise use **-lar**.

Person	Kişi	Adjective	Sıfat
Afghan(s)	**Afganistanlı(lar)**	Afghan	**Afgan**
Albanian(s)	**Arnavut(lar)**	Albanian	**Arnavut**
Algerian(s)	**Cezayirli(ler)**	Algerian	**Cezayirli**
American(s)	**Amerikalı(lar)**	American	**Amerikan**
Argentine(s)	**Arjantinli(ler)**	Argentine	**Arjantinli**
Armenian(s)	**Ermeni(ler)**	Armenian	**Ermeni**
Australian(s)	**Avustralyalı(lar)**	Australian	**Avustralyalı**
Austrian(s)	**Avusturyalı(lar)**	Austrian	**Avusturyalı**
Azerbaijani(s)	**Azerbaycanlı(lar)**	Azerbaijani	**Azeri**
Belgian(s)	**Belçikalı(lar)**	Belgian	**Belçikalı**
Bolivian(s)	**Bolivyalı(lar)**	Bolivian	**Bolivyalı**
Brazilian(s)	**Brezilyalı(lar)**	Brazilian	**Brezilyalı**
Bulgarian(s)	**Bulgaristanlı(lar)**	Bulgarian	**Bulgar**
Canadian(s)	**Kanadalı(lar)**	Canadian	**Kanadalı**
Chinese (sing.& pl.)	**Çinli(ler)**	Chinese	**Çinli**
Colombian(s)	**Kolombiyalı(lar)**	Colombian	**Kolombiyalı**
Cuban(s)	**Kübalı(lar)**	Cuban	**Kübalı**
Cypriot(s)	**Kıbrıslı(lar)**	Cypriot	**Kıbrıslı**
Czech(s)	**Çekoslovak(lar)** **Çekoslovakyalı(lar)**	Czech	**Çek**
Dane(s)	**Danimarkalı(lar)**	Danish	**Danimarkalı**
Dutchman (men), Dutchwoman (women)	**Hollandalı(lar)**	Dutch	**Hollandalı**
Egyptian(s)	**Mısırlı(lar)**	Egyptian	**Mısırlı**
Briton British (pl.) an English man an English woman	**İngiliz(ler)**	British	**İngiliz**
Finn(s)	**Finli(ler)**	Finnish	**Fin**

Person	**Kişi**	**Adjective**	**Sıfat**
Frenchman (men), Frenchwoman (women)	**Fransız(lar)**	French	**Fransız**
German(s)	**Alman(lar)**	German	**Alman**
Greek(s)	**Yunanlı(lar)**	Greek	**Yunan / Yunanlı**
Hungarian(s)	**Macar(lar)**	Hungarian	**Macar**
Indian(s)	**Hintli(ler)**	Indian	**Hintli**
Indonesian(s)	**Endonezyalı(lar)**	Indonesian	**Endonez**
Iranian(s)	**İranlı(lar)**	Iranian	**İranlı**
Iraqi(s)	**Iraklı(lar)**	Iraqi	**Iraklı**
Irishwoman(women) Irishman (men) Irish (pl.)	**İrlandalı(lar)**	Irish	**İrlandalı**
Israeli(s)	**İsrailli(ler)**	Israeli	**İsrailli**
Italian(s)	**İtalyan(lar)**	Italian	**İtalyan**
Japanese (sing.&pl.)	**Japon(lar)**	Japanese	**Japon**
Jordanian(s)	**Ürdünlü(ler)**	Jordanian	**Ürdünlü**
Kazakhstani(s)	**Kazak(lar)**	Kazakhstani	**Kazak**
Korean(s)	**Koreli(ler)**	Korean	**Koreli**
Kyrgyz(s) / Kyrgyzstani(s)	**Kırgız(lar)**	Kyrgyz / Kyrgyzstani	**Kırgız**
Lebanese (sing.&pl.)	**Lübnanlı(lar)**	Lebanese	**Lübnanlı**
Libyan(s)	**Libyalı(lar)**	Libyan	**Libyalı**
Mexican(s)	**Meksikalı(lar)**	Mexican	**Meksikalı**
Norwegian(s)	**Norveçli(ler)**	Norwegian	**Norveçli**
Pole(s)	**Polonyalı(lar)**	Polish	**Polonyalı**
Portuguese(sing.&pl.)	**Portekizli(ler)**	Portuguese	**Portekizli**
Romanian(s)	**Romen(ler) / Romanyalı(lar)**	Romanian	**Romen**
Russian(s)	**Rus(lar)**	Russian	**Rus**
Saudi(s)	**Suidi(ler) / Arap(lar)**	Saudi / Saudi Arabian	**Arap**
Serb(s)	**Sırp(lar)**	Serbian	**Sırp / Sırplı**
South African(s)	**Güney Afrikalı(lar)**	South African	**Güney Afrikalı**

Person	**Kişi**	**Adjective**	**Sıfat**
Spaniard(s)	**İspanyol(lar)**	Spanish	**İspanyol**
Swede(s)	**İsveçli(ler)**	Swedish	**İsveçli**
Swiss (sing. & pl.)	**İsviçreli(ler)**	Swiss	**İsviçreli**
Syrian(s)	**Suriyeli(ler)**	Syrian	**Suriyeli**
Tajikistani(s)	**Tacikistanlı(lar)**	Tajikistani	**Tacik**
Tunisian(s)	**Tunuslu(lar)**	Tunisian	**Tunuslu**
Turk(s)	**Türk(ler)**	Turkish	**Türk**
Turkmen(s)	**Türkmenistanlı(lar)**	Turkmen	**Türkmen**
Uzbekistani(s)	**Özbekistanlı(lar)**	Uzbekistani	**Özbek**
Venezuelan(s)	**Venezüellalı(lar)**	Venezuelan	**Venezüellalı**

International Trade Terms

[Import/Export]

Uluslararası Ticari Terimler Sözlüğü [İthalat / İhracat]

In this section, you will find a glossary of international trade terms. However, most of import-export terms are in English in international treading affairs. Traders usually can understand you without having to speak any Turkish. Here are some expressions you will find useful to know.

acceptance	**onaylama / uygun bulma**
account	**banka hesabı / kar / hesap**
amendment	**düzeltme / değişiklik**
carriage and insurance paid to **[CIP]**	**sigorta+adrese teslim**
carriage paid to **[CPT]**	**adrese teslim**
cash	**peşin para, nakit**
cash against documents **[CAD]**	**vesaik mukabili**
cash against goods **[CAG]**	**mal mukabili**
cash in advance	**peşin**
cash price	**peşin fiyatı**
cash up front	**peşin ödeme**
cost and freight [**CFR** / c&f]	**mal bedeli + nakliye**
cost, insurance and freight **[CIF]**	**mal bedeli + sigorta pirimi + nakliye**
customs broker	**gümrük komisyoncusu**
customs declaration	**gümrük beyannamesi**
customs duty	**gümrük vergisi**
deferred L/C	**vadeli akreditif**
delivered at frontier **[DAF]**	**sınırda teslim**
delivered duty paid **[DDP]**	**gümrük ödenmiş teslim**
delivered duty unpaid **[DDU]**	**gümrüksüz teslim**
delivered ex quay (Duty Paid) **[DEQ]**	**rıhtımda gümrük ödenerek teslim**
delivered ex ship [DES]	**gemi güvertesinde teslim**
delivered ex works	**işyerinde teslim**
draft	**poliçe**
drawee	**muhatap / alıcı**
drawer	**satıcı**
dumping	**damping**
duty free	**gümrükten muaf**

duty paid	**gümrüklü**
ex works **[EXW]**	**işyerinde teslim**
export permit	**ihracat belgesi**
export quotas	**kota**
free alongside ship **[FAS]**	**gemi bordasında teslim**
free carrier **[FCA]** (named port)	**taşıyıcıya teslim**
free on board **[FOB]**	**gemi güvertesinde teslim**
free on board airport (fob airport)	**havaalanında teslim**
gross domestic / national product (GDP/GNP)	**gayrı safi milli hasıla / gayrı safi milli gelir**
in advance	**peşin ödeme**
L/C at sight	**görüldüğünde ödemeli akreditif**
letter of credit **[L/C]**	**akreditif**
open account	**açık hesap**
payee	**alacaklı**
protest	**protesto**
tariff	**gümrük tarifesi**